# The Philosophy of Doublethink

## Theory of Contradictory Values

*by Rick Weires*

*Asbury House Publishing Company*
ASBURY, IOWA

Carry on Wayward Son
Words and Music by Kerry Livgren
© 1976 EMI BLACKWOOD MUSIC INC. and DON KIRSHNER MUSIC
All Rights Controlled and Administered by EMI BLACKWOOD MUSIC INC.
All Rights Reserved    International Copyright Secured    Used by Permission

5:15
The Seeker
Written by Pete Townshend
© Towser Tunes, Inc. (BMI)/ Abkco Music Inc./ Fabulous Music
All rights for the world on behalf of Towser Tunes Inc. (BMI) administered by
BMG Music Publishing International Ltd. (PRS)
All rights for the US on behalf of BMG Music Publishing International Ltd.
(PRS) administered by Careers-BMG Music Publishing, Inc. (BMI)

First printing 2005

ISBN 0-9754893-4-8          LCCN 2004106220

*To my patient wife Karen,
for putting up with a very
distracted husband over the past
several years. Thank you.*

*To my friend and original
co-creator of doublethink.*

# Table of Contents

# Introduction

*People who lean on logic and philosophy and rational exposition end by starving the best part of the mind.*

—J. B. YEATES

---

What kind of person writes the book on mental anarchy attempting to unravel philosophy? Probably not the person you are imagining. My life so far has been ordinary by most standards. I am a husband, father of three, and an engineer who works on safety and electrical issues for a large Midwestern manufacturer. The main quirk in my lifestyle is that I study an unusual selection of books on existentialism, behaviorism, cognativism, and psychoanalysis.

The odd combination, electrical engineer with a strong interest in psychology and philosophy, inevitably leads me to notice differences between minds, philosophies, and silicon-based logic. If you were to step into my shoes, with my perspective, you would immediately be stricken by the disparity. During the day I review electrical designs based on modern digital electronic circuits, which force values to cold sterile repeatable absolutes—yes or no, true or false, 1 or 0. And then at home during the evenings, I study human thought processes, which are roughly chemically-analog based, emotionally laden, and highly unpredictable. Despite these fundamental differences, strangely both minds and microprocessors somehow manage to perform many similar tasks, including adding numbers, manipulating objects, and remembering things.

But if they function so much the same in certain ways, why is it that I never see the equivalent of common mental mishaps occurring on computers and other electronic devices? For example, I have yet to witness a calculator's judgment impaired by anger, nor have I ever heard of a distressed Dell laptop verbally assaulting an Apple iBook. I am quite certain that VCRs do not fall in love with DVD players. Really the question I am getting at is, how do all of the anxious and aroused states in humans so drastically alter their ability to think rationally, but yet these same states never hold sway over microprocessors? What makes us humans and not robots?

If you are still as biased as I was in noticing these kinds of mental flaws, you might hope to find logically based explanations to account for the lapses in human reasoning. But once you carefully compare functions between a near-perfect binary machine and emotional organic being, you may throw in the towel. Becoming frustrated because of numerous issues discussed throughout this book, I eventually abandoned the sensible approach to understanding thinking and started from scratch.

With little else to go on I turned to the philosophers, scanning for those with less than purely reasoned outlooks. But which of the philosophers would dare to start with the premise that human behavior did not have to make any sense? Ironically, late in the process of writing this book I found one of the earliest from ancient Greece, Pyrrho of Elis (circa 360–270 B.C.). Very little is known of this man, but it was rumored that he grew so skeptical of knowledge, others had to follow him about. His disbelief in everything, including the things he saw, inclined him to walk into dangers. Pyrrho and his fellow skeptics "were constantly engaged in overthrowing the dogmas of all schools, but annunciated none themselves…laid down nothing definitely, not even the laying down of nothing" (Diog. Laert. 9.62, 9.74).

Certainly Pyrrho's outlook sounds quite silly to most, but whether you agree with it or not, he raised the key issue of this book: What do we know for sure? Unfortunately for the philosophical world, the way he formulated his problem scared most of the sensible people away; he started with the assumption that the solution was impossible by definition, giving little incentive for those that followed. The rival camps of Pyrrho's approximate era, namely Plato and Aristotle, offered more appealing rational approaches. Those two Greeks were under some sort of illusion that the world could be described in a more neat, orderly, and consistent system. And this is, after all, what we usually desire. Because Pyrrho's uncertainty creates stress and anguish, I believe it explains why you'll not find much positive recognition of him and the skeptics beyond ancient Greece nor for the ensuing 2,200 years.

But after the two millennia drought, you should note the existentialist philosophers beginning in the nineteenth century. Three of them in particular carry a similar basic theme: Fyodor Dostoyevsky, Friedrich Nietzsche, and Sigmund Freud. Starting with the first, I read book after book by the Russian and found him fully competent at tearing apart moral structure and exposing inconsistency in reason. He liberated me from pretense with frank portrayals of parenticide, gambling, and prostitution. He delivered insight while examining the awful realities of human nature. His perspective from a brutal nineteenth century Russia was  never meant to reassure (again this is obvious to anyone who's ever read his detailed accounts of thievery, loan sharking, disease, and so forth). Nonetheless his novels allowed me to overcome the fear of my own vile thoughts and see clearly what compromises I made to create a world consistent with my superficial perceptions. Additionally, he fostered severe and unhealthy skepticism for the people in my life; in particular I noticed everyone seemed to be hiding some awful plot or opinion inside, while meekly acting like all was normal on the outside.

Just because Dostoyevsky successfully identified the problem did not justify his excessive pessimism. Why would a man with so much insight dwell in such misery? Although I admire his integrity in understanding the flaws of human character, I have never felt compelled to follow in his destructive lifestyle. (It is interesting to note he too was an engineer with a passion for psychology and philosophy.)

I also turned to the writings of Friedrich Nietzsche. Once again I discovered the bottom of my soul and how wrong I can be about everything. Declaring God dead as well as his utter contempt for the philosophy of his day, Nietzsche called on me to rise above the herd instinct of the ordinary men, and lead them—he gave me the 'overman' or 'superman' (Nietzsche [1892] 1978, 3, 4). He was at least trying to leave something positive and concrete, but from my perspective, he too failed as a guide. Intermixed with the 'overman' was his brand of extreme pessimism and general sense of disgust with Christian feebleness. He provided me little incentive to adopt this outlook. Knowing he went insane and inspired many a Nazi does not speak well of his positions either. Nonetheless he did attack the inconsistencies most other philosophers ignore, penetrated the masquerade of rational philosophy, and exposed what lies behind the curtain of philosophical mythology.

Frustrated throughout the inquiry, I kept returning to Freud. There was no boundary he could not cross for the purpose of knowledge and empiricism, confronting the anxieties of our mixed-up world. Although he lacked the viciousness of Dostoyevsky and Nietzsche, he still managed to tear down moral confines, openly discussing molestation, abuse, and fears of castration. Unfortunately when Freud tried to reassemble the mind according to his new understanding, he was often simply wrong—and incomplete. Freud provided a path for me to follow but then he too failed to deliver. (I do not wish to sound arrogant and judge him harshly [or the others for that matter] when in fact he demonstrated pro-

4

found insight and genius. Freudian perspectives on dreams, anxiety, and psychoanalysis were revolutionary; it is just that we have other options and should strive to do so much more.)

And then in the middle of the philosophical mess from an unlikely source, I took notice of the term "doublethink," found in the book *1984* by George Orwell. If you like a riddle to challenge yourself with, you should hold tight to Orwell until you resolve his. In the beginning most will still value finding a consistent philosophical path, but the blatancy of the lie that is doublethink haunts you. The very notion clearly admits to lying, telling you it is going to lie, and indeed it does lie—a lie you will come to depend upon if you succeed in your journey. Here it is captured in Orwell's own eloquent words:

> ...use conscious deception while retaining the firmness of purpose that goes with complete honesty. To tell deliber- ate lies while genuinely believing them, to forget any fact that has become inconvenient, and then, when it becomes necessary again, to draw it back from oblivion for just so long as it is needed, to deny the existence of the objective reality and all the while to take into account of the reality which one denies—all this is indispensably necessary. Even in using the word doublethink it is necessary to exercise doublethink. For by using the word one admits that one is tampering with reality; by a fresh act of doublethink one erases this knowl- edge; and so on indefinitely, with the lie always one leap ahead of the truth (Orwell [1949] 1983, 176–177).

Life always creates more riddles than answers, and upon this particular mystery, you may ponder for decades before finding the answers. The solution, it turns out, is a whole other perspective on life. Orwell created his paradox solely on the ordinary blind faith approach to logic; he led his read- ers to the brink, yet did not take them to the other side. Orwell wanted others to tremble, never knowing what was lurking behind the facade of common sense.

In Orwell's gloomy doublethinking society, deception provides the basis for the totalitarian government. Officially sponsored doublethink smothers logic, structure, and order—leading to hopeless despair. Big Brother watches over as the government twists the mind around. The propaganda machine mangles as well as manipulates every thought, eventually abolishing all truth including the fundamentals of reasoning. This deliberate misuse of logic often turns on itself. To make matters worse no sensible answers are ever found. In the end, Orwell showed no useful purpose, nor any salvation for doublethinking, only describing the angst it caused.

In contrast to this bleak and overwhelmingly negative impression, you will need to consider another perspective: doublethink—the philosophy of the not-so-Orwellian variety, embracing confusion and disarray. (Note: Doublethink will have multiple meanings in this book. Sometimes it will describe a philosophy, sometimes it will mean confusion, and sometimes it will imply criticism of the inconsistencies found in other philosophies. Usually it will combine connotations of all three.) On the following pages are documented ironclad evidence of pervasive mixed-up thinking. Once established, confusion provides a starting point, in doublethink the only possible one; any other beginning proves twice as absurd.

But using confusion as a platform will not quickly endear this philosophy to even slightly rational beings, since mental anguish follows those who say, "I am both right and wrong in this matter. I shall move ahead with my decision to love and hate, despite the fact that I am completely misled and headed for destruction by my poor decisions. However, others shall recognize me as the only one who understood, while succeeding with luck on my side."

Life contradicts itself, and even if the overwhelming proof demonstrated throughout this book supports the acceptance of bewilderment, only a few will openly declare: "I am beautiful, ugly, smart, stupid, evil, as well as good. Furthermore the path to happiness relies upon lying, stealing, giving, sharing, hating, or loving; which also establishes the route to misery filled with despair."

Learning to accept absurdity requires great courage, but you cannot truly live life without going nose to nose with being so wrong. Every aspect of thought baffles and mixes itself up. Doublethink the philosophy takes the obvious logical steps no other sensible or educated person has ever taken. It answers questions most normal people never even ask. (Granted the results at times leave one totally unsatisfied.) Doublethink is the only solution that resolves issues consistently from the easiest up to the most complex: "Stealing is cruel, kind, and not a moral question. Love is beautiful, desirable, sick, and humiliating. God is dead, alive, evil, good, incoherent, ugly, terrible, tender, kind, and compassionate."

Doublethink challenges every conviction, as well as feeling. What the reader once found comfortably acceptable becomes a flat-out abomination. It explores where nothing has ever been seen before, finding new ideas, picking up the overlooked and ignored, then giving new meaning, eventually challenging everything that exists.

Doublethink promotes underhanded goals—even the devil shows more consistency. Doublethink turns on itself, allowing lies with distortions; indeed, it thrives upon them. Right blurs into wrong, while values bend to accommodate, and clear ideas grow fuzzy. Sharp distinctions slowly round, making such morphing appear desirable.

Rationalization takes on a whole other meaning, while morals are set free to seek out good or evil. All types of control collapse, leaving no beliefs in a solid form. Doublethink accounts to no principles, not even its own. Confining the nonsensical beast presents an impossible task. You can't pick it up or hold it down; instead it cracks your core human values, turning your mind inside out.

Doublethink, the philosophy, invites disgust and terror. At first tugging the heart in all directions, it unravels the fabric of ethical systems, shuffling the deck, mixing ideas with thoughts; and then while forcing a painful look inside the mind, it whips emotions around, causing horrible anguish. Its inconsistencies are nearly impossible to accept as it wriggles like a worm through garbage, searching for a speck of food. It smashes the mind apart exposing the spiritual foundation, brashly never giving support nor rationalization. It lacks reason, exuding only ambition; anything short of upsetting anarchy simply indicates a lack of understanding; it disturbs by necessity.

# 1 *Doublethinking:* *Intentionally Confusing the Mind*

*I have values, but I don't know how or why.*
—THE WHO, "THE SEEKER"

*If the following chapter irritates, unnerves, and angers you, then read it all. If you find it cathartic as I do, then read it again and again. Digest it slowly, allowing your mind to fill with images of contradictions. The many examples provided create a backbone for conflicted thought. Your job is to fill in the details by painting a picture inside your mind. Visualize the events described actually occurring. Place yourself, friends, neighbors, relatives, and coworkers in the various situations. Once the event seems real and concrete, move quickly to the next. Although the task seems impossible at first, later, with practice, you'll discover you can do it.*

*On the other hand, portions of or perhaps all the contents of this chapter may never register with some readers. Do not worry if this is the case for you; it is not essential for the understanding of most of the rest of this book. I still encourage the disinterested or bored reader to try to remain open minded, but if nothing here gets you riled up, read it once and move ahead.*

The dictionary defines philosophy as the love of knowledge. This definition implies a benefit from gaining more understanding. Furthermore the dictionary's meaning assumes a certain inherent desirability in logic, consistency, and reason. In light of the doublethink philosophy, this explanation really does not work. Doublethink redefines the thought process, breaking down logic.

Specifically it:

- Believes two desperate bank robbers' alibis, even though numerous eyewitnesses dispute them and willingly testify in court.

- Treats a three-year-old's explanation of photosynthesis as the basis for a series of tests to confirm trees are green because giants color them that way.

- Claims expert government testimony on foreign policy validates the legitimacy of corruption and theft.

- Pursues certain political agendas because they promote poverty, war, and anarchy.

- Treats a philosophical proposition, like mind-body dualism, as legitimate when modern psychology determines otherwise.

- Acts as though hangover-induced vomiting and headaches result from something besides the intake of excessive amounts of alcohol.

- Daydreams about power, then believes in the fantasy of being in control of a small African country.

- Laughs at the death of a small innocent girl.

- Fears a gentle, white fluffy lamb.

- Encourages teaching grammar school students the details of successful colon surgery.

- Denies an affair with a seductive eighteen-year-old neighbor—after your wife already called her own lawyer.

- Tells the truth about a magic trick when deceit provides better entertainment for the audience.

Doublethink applauds Don Quixote slaying windmills because they are dragons. Doublethink approves depriving the mind of the obvious. Doublethink is:

- Pretending rain falling on the ground dries the grass and flowers.
- Asking nonsensical questions such as why ducks talk or fish eat large stones.
- Trying to prove triangles are squared off circles.
- Justifying stealing a red car as opposed to a yellow one.
- Making decisions about sex without considering the possibility of contracting syphilis.
- Denying camels dwell in desert countries despite seeing pictures clearly showing camels crossing sand dunes.
- Ignoring the bloody knife and stab wounds at the crime scene, thus making asphyxiation the only possible cause of death.
- Checking the Oxford dictionary in hopes of finding the incorrect spelling of "toad."

Doublethink encourages a man to intentionally deceive himself. In particular, doublethink promotes the following acts:

- Believing in the love of God, while acting on behalf of the devil.
- Walking aimlessly into a busy street expecting to not be run over.
- Going to a seven-dollar movie with only fifty cents.
- Arguing to have the price raised on the house you intend to buy.
- Driving east to end up farther north.
- Explaining that a drinking problem is due to the high cost of education.
- Avoiding a heart attack by eating greasy doughnuts.

- Extending credit to a company without collateral, knowing it is about to file for bankruptcy.
- Picking sunflowers in a field of tulips.
- Getting drunk with friends after an Alcoholics Anonymous meeting.
- Playing a piano with no keys or broken keys.

Doublethink puts together ideas that do not fit together. A study of doublethink, however, reveals still other facets, such as keeping company with the conspicuous and not-so-subtle followers of absurdity. Doublethink:

- Treats foolishness as wisdom.
- Trades sanity for silliness.
- Chooses casino gambling over guaranteed wealth.
- Wishes for a drug overdose when life has finally straightened itself out.
- Creates a place where dogs become fish, and vice-versa.

Doublethink accepts the anguish created by empty thoughts, even when correct answers reside nearby. Doublethink:

- Promotes fear of monsters, goblins, and other mythical beasts.
- Jokes about apprehensive painful thoughts.
- Solves math problems to lower the total score on a quiz.
- Believes plagiarism promotes creativity because reality fell asleep.
- Twists knowledge of higher reasoning into madness.
- Breaks the laws of physics including gravity.
- Thinks psychic powers of ants promote sensuality.

Doublethink unsettles. Say God exists then advocate atheism, or that black is white, while white is black. Finally it assumes:

- Down points up, up heads over, followed by over going out.
- Abortionists murder, and yet money justifies euthanasia in all instances.
- Stealing from the rich seems acceptable provided the thief already owns hundreds of diamonds set in gold.
- Black people appear inferior to Africans, but northern Europeans look superior to Caucasians.
- Politicians live filthy wretched existences, yet deserve equal protection under the law.

Absurdity and logic grow from the same tree. Inside travels outside while outside walks upside-down. Green chooses yellow and purple matches red. Alice's adventures in wonderland become curiouser and curiouser. Cold weather feels warm as cattle eat beans. The pope professes Judaism while nonsense begot logic. Five plus five equals twelve and a half.

Doublethink the philosophy does not confuse looking at criminals from a different perspective. For example, the rapist and the woman raped will explain the event in different ways, despite the fact that only one assault took place. One's perspective, however, defines doublethink. The bottom side of a car looks very different from the top side, even though a single car possesses both a top and bottom. This explains little about doublethink, and still a person's point of view encompasses every aspect of doublethink.

If this book no longer makes sense then instability will start producing a new kind of reasoning. An unpeeled apple tastes like a banana. A rotten orange smells like an orange. Music consists of Bach, Beethoven, and bean soup. Pigs make veal because chickens lay ham. Pleasant equals justice; abhorrent corresponds to evil, but consistency avoids logic, while a false pregnancy test is not always welcome.

Finding integrity requires illogic. Justice seeks both right and wrong verdicts. Poor structure can't legitimize nihilism, because erroneous belief systems take precedence. But being true has nothing to do with the world; therefore all rationalization proves false by default. If correspondence has nothing to do with being correct or off kilter, it definitely possesses meaning. Until the confusion abounds, understanding fails. When chaos runs free then common sense will follow. Ideas take time to absorb—yet they float both in and out of the mind.

Doublethink implies two meanings, while exposing garbage. A person is absolutely right as he goes insane. But that judgment seems premature, because it essentially assumes understanding based on lies. If all answers were available, I would lay them out for the reader's benefit; since they exist nearby, they remain ambiguous. Basically everything stated conflicts. All thoughts contradict themselves—or at least they lie to some extent.

The enlightened doublethinker must consider both options simultaneously. He or she should act as though ideas contain right together with wrong. The individual seeking the greatest wisdom holds sympathy for contradictory causes. The optimally confused intellectual invests in both winning and losing an issue as well as feeling the pain of exactness and sloppiness at the same time. The victor in this game embraces the joy of acting consistent, despite the total lack of evidence supporting a coherent understanding of the issue.

The most useful result of doublethink is positively explaining everything while at the same time clarifying drivel. That also illustrates the least practical feature of doublethink. Doublethink first triumphs over structure and then attacks coherence.

Doublethink welcomes disorder, chaos, anarchy, riots, decay, emptiness, anxiety, fear, terror, isolation, pain, crying, frustration, and sadness. At the same time doublethink fights for order, structure, civility, peace, preservation, fullness, calm, confidence, kindness, camaraderie, pleasure, laughing, success, happiness, and righteousness.

Lies and distortion cover the paper, which lacks numbers on the pages. Paragraphs slip in to phrases, periods. Full sentences prove useless in the attempt to express a total disregard of the English language. Nothing escapes the wrath of doublethink. Its emptiness permeates the basic principles of communication. It falls into blabber…Aasss sssssssssss06387 9fdgaiou agjfag j96lkj0u9 gggfjopu-08u- nmmm 9qua:)@% &*%#(APHI D%$KHFHF ldfagas Doublethink has reason, focus, and energy. a;ljgffff fffffffff ffffffffff fffffffffffffffffff ffff fffff ffffff ffffffffffd dddddd dddddddd ddddd dddd

# 2 *Self-Deception:*
## *The Unavoidable Confusion*

*Oh, what a tangled web we weave,*
*when first we practice to deceive!*

—SIR WALTER SCOTT

Doublethink sickens many readers at this point. After all, who in their right mind utters the muck written in chapter one? Who besides a fallen angel promotes and thrives on pure subversion? What boundary protects a mind consumed with conflicting versions of reality? What remains untouched? Why wish for a mental collapse?

Well, in many respects, the answers to those questions do not matter.

Chapter two, and other later chapters, will demonstrate that doublethink, while hiding in the background, allows no more option than sleep. The motives clearly exist to doublethink, the mind accepts doublethink, and furthermore the indications suggest doublethink occurs in many situations. To understand this common and naturally occurring form of doublethink, I have modeled the mind fooling itself with the following observations.

1. There exist many desires that are difficult to obtain and cannot be fulfilled.
2. We sometimes become desperate.

17

3. The mind possesses the ability to deceive itself.
4. The mind will deceive itself if convinced dishonesty helps obtain the object desired.

The first observation provides motives. There are lots of obvious reasons for self-deception, including those that are social, personal, economic, religious, philosophical, and medical in nature. Motives for a person tricking him- or herself can be anything strongly desired but not easily obtained. The following instances illustrate such cases. (Note: The names used in personal examples throughout this book are completely fictitious except when I speak of myself or of famous individuals.)

# Observation Number One

## *Jim Conner*

Jim Conner closes his eyes and sees the television cameras chasing his car as if he were hauling a youthful English princess. He fantasizes about cruising through town in a 2005 red BMW convertible, hour after hour swerving to miss the paparazzi, cameras flashing, blinding his eyes.

After all the evasive driving he finally loses the media swarm, and lifts his cell phone to his ear to hear a desperate young actress on the other end, wishing to see him again this evening. The naughty mistress Leeza, simply refuses to wait until the weekend as planned, but must arrange for a rendezvous this very night. Jim recalls her soft, long, light brown curled hair, remembers previous sexual encounters—but suddenly grows tired of this scene and decides he can do better calling a different and more attractive lady friend. Absentmindedly still making the phone connection, he pulls into a gas station where the attendant instantly recognizes the famous bachelor and asks Mr. Conner politely for an autograph.

Unfortunately for Jim, wishing for wealth and fame has left him empty-handed and resentful. His real world does not quit live up to continuous parties and wild orgies (all funded by an endless stream of cash). Jim lives in a small studio apartment that needs to have all the smoke stained walls repainted as well as the carpet steam cleaned. For dinner the lonely bachelor sifts through the empty boxes of pizza on the kitchen table until finding one with a small thumping object bouncing around inside. Hoping to eat a slice of day-old sausage pizza, he raises the lid to discover a plastic saltshaker lying on its side and six small black ants scrambling for cover.

Depressed, hungry, and out of money again because of a recent involuntary job change, Jim contemplates his situation. The last restaurant manager expected employees to work every other Friday evening, while previous egotistical maniacs have demanded busboys show up for work clean and neatly dressed, at least five days per week. These unbearable control freaks just never compromise to the point where working long hard hours is not required.

The angry daydreamer continues to grasp for more money than he can obtain, creating a vision that clashes with reality. Jim doesn't have a clue about how to earn truckloads of cash, but rather finds it easier to fantasize about the rich and famous, instead of improving upon his job skills and work performance. Clearly he could do better, but he fears that the added effort is simply not worth it.

The neighbors complain about the sulfur aroma seeping from beneath his apartment door. The women he so longs for never follow him home (for obvious reasons). Perhaps several ways exist to improve his condition, but the point remains the same: He is totally unsatisfied with life, while the situation keeps getting worse. Jim possesses little of what he deems worthy to live for, in part because, poor depressed single men have all the motives needed to doublethink; they prefer make-believing about rich guy utopia instead of going through all the trouble of trying to fix the real problems.

(His strong desires are numerous: cash, sex, prestige, respect, a better home, and fame.)

## Karen Johnson

Karen lives in a very different situation. With her only child's philandering father absent and high on marijuana, she alone endures the burden of raising their troubled sixteen-year-old boy. Two months ago on a Saturday evening the prodigal son, Robert, stole a bottle of Captain Morgan Rum, drove her minivan across the Mississippi river into Illinois. Once there he promptly ran into a parked Ford Taurus, before stumbling into the brush behind the nightclub parking lot. Wasting no time the local police department promptly encircled the perimeter of the vacant lot and closed in on Karen's hiding child. She became aware of the activity when she received a desperate call at 3 A.M. Sunday. A few days later she picked him up and brought him home.

Karen appreciated the fact that Robert spent three nights and days in the county jail with plenty of time for contemplating what he did wrong, how he hurt his mother, and where his life is headed. She's not stupid and knows he enjoys the wild nightlife, but now he also knows more about the inside of jail cell and his new unsavory friends than he cares to.

Today (two months after the incarceration) we find Karen once again in a state of anguish, this time about how much drinking might still occur. In particular Karen faces two ideas that contradict. Her son promises he will go to his best friend's high school graduation party, but not touch the rum, vodka, whisky…. However, his recent escapades have established a pattern of drinking at parties then lying to avoid punishment. The jail sentence might have cured the problem or maybe not. Karen wants a resolution for this dilemma, but if she chooses the wrong course of action she runs high risks. She may either further alienate her misbehaving offspring—or worse, she may need to identify his corpse after a car wreck on US 20. How much more tension can a parent have? This time she lets him go, but the choice provides little relief from the anxiety.

## Dr. Steven M.

Dr. M., a physician for a large suburban Chicago nursing home, cares for an elderly patient nearing death. This particular patient suffers a great deal of joint pain caused by arthritis, and he no longer behaves in a civil manner. The despondent pain-killer-dazed senior citizen recently requested that his eldest daughter not visit. He doesn't want that ungrateful snot anywhere near his room. Caught in the middle, Steve obsesses over whether to respect the wishes of a dying man or ignore the confused ranting coming out of the mouth of a stressed-out grouch.

The doctor's interest in doing the *best* helps maintain his reputation as an ethical physician. Steven also attends physicians' conferences on the aging and even sits on the board directors for a church-sponsored retirement community. Unfortunately all this effort fails to resolve the current dilemma, because although the good doctor listens at each meeting and conference, little time is spent covering the finer details of bedside manner for grumpy old men. He lacks the information needed to make his choice with confidence.

This morning, before leaving for work, Steve's wife Laura added another upsetting incident to his worries. Mrs. M. reminded Steve that she expects him to share the burden of raising their children. Specifically she noted how infrequently he arrives home before the supper table has been cleared, stinging him particularly hard since he feels strongly that both a man and a woman must help each other with the upbringing of their children. Spending late evenings making the rounds and filling out paperwork at the hospital in no way encourages Steven's son to learn to read, or makes certain the baths are taken before 7:30 P.M., or even that Santa Claus buys the correct books and toy trucks. Clearly work exhaustion prevents the diligent doctor from spending the daily hours required for properly raising intelligent, well-mannered children. But he also needs to take the important time for helping his aged acquaintances.

In Steven's case we find the sources for the tension mixed, and with an additive affect. Both dilemmas build on each other, raising the net effect on his judgment ever higher. He finds no peace at work, nor any at home, only despair everywhere. How reliable could his judgment be under such circumstances? How clearly does a man think with the burden of caring for less than sane elderly patients, while fending off the attacks of less than understanding wife?

## *Albert Fischer*

Christians claim a paradise above welcomes the faithful; atheists say nothing but clouds fill the sky; agnostics like Albert languish in doubtful gloom. He wishes for everlasting joy but insists on completely certain knowledge. Fueling the doubt is a local businessman who maintains faith in God consists of nonsensical superstition. Owning a large successful factory as well as the respect of the community, this entrepreneur defiantly rejects God and calls the faithful mentally weak do-gooders. Albert suspiciously asks himself why God blesses this heathen with so much wealth. Why not make the nonbeliever more average, more ordinary? Why does the community heap praise on one so isolated from God? Why does God not set an example and make the do-gooders have the large houses and fast boats instead?

Most importantly, Albert really wants confidence that the decisions he makes in life will get him to heaven, and that he is not wasting his Sunday mornings listening to sermons about a carpenter and some fishermen, when he could be enjoying himself. He admits a great comfort would come from knowing eternal bliss awaits those who follow the Lord's teachings. So you might ask, why not make a choice to believe and be done with it? Because some people like Albert still think a lie is a lie. If it turns out there was no God, he would be following a false illusion, not the savior.

Albert and the other undecided live their lives in fruitless searches for a way to understand God's existence. They find the teachings in the Bible vague and uncertain, and the rules often burdensome and painful. If there were no heaven they could have a lot more fun, stop giving money to the church, and enjoy casual sex from time to time, but never have to feel guilty. They look at what the believer must give up and say, "Is it possible they are wasting their precious time on earth, following a fictitious Bible?" Naturally with so much at stake, it pulls their emotions in many directions. Albert and his kind envy those who can decide and live at peace. They just wish they knew.

## Observation Number Two

All the above examples show desires unfulfilled. Contradictions and conflicts such as these come in an infinite variety, constantly battling inside our minds causing great stress. In many cases the above examples could essentially go away and never lead to doublethink. A man like Jim Conner could accept his fate, remain poor, and never think about what he really wants. But other times the mind puts forth extraordinary means chasing the desired outcome. Item two in the self-deception model begins the struggle to address these problems, stating that we sometimes act desperately.

### *Karen Johnson 11*

Karen's problem's with her son are compounded by the fact that she recently found her husband Tim sleeping with another woman. The lousy whore's affair with her man went on for at least three months. The thinner, younger marriage-wrecker works in the same office as Tim, while she the jealous spouse grows more and more humiliated to the point she can barely leave the house to buy groceries. She had spent years attending office Christmas parties with all the people now familiar with the intimate details of Tim's betrayal. So angry and hurt, she purchased a used semiautomatic pistol, not certain if it would be used to shoot Tim, the whore, or herself.

Perhaps it means little now, but her guilty partner weeps with sorrow, wanting to make up for his mistakes. He said the office affair meant nothing and that his wife and marriage now matter most. Despite the fact that she will never believe Tim again, Karen's racing mind cannot decide what to do. Should she take Tim back? Will he mess around again? Is she a fool? When does the pain go away?

Tim's lies hurt so badly, and making matters worse Karen cries the nights away alone in their king-sized waterbed staring at the oak dresser her betrayer built. Karen ponders everything about their relationship, the day they met, the long-stemmed red roses he bought her, the evening they first made love, and the last time she saw him (in the very same matching oak waterbed with that red-haired concubine). She desperately seeks resolution of this crisis, but so far there are no obvious ways to make the pain stop.

## Karen Johnson III

We come to Karen once more. We already know she is separated, raising a son, and now we see stress compounded by a weight problem. She sincerely believes that if she lost twenty-five pounds she would regain her confidence. She started dieting several years ago, but failed miserably. Typically Karen loses a few pounds and then she falls apart. For example, at 10:30 last night she walked through the kitchen heard her stomach scream at her. Whenever Karen passes near the refrigerator, she opens the door and feasts on the first leftovers she can find. Karen conditioned herself by responding to hunger, or in other words, do whatever it takes to get any remaining morsels of food.

Over the last two years Karen began experimenting with increasingly severe measures of losing weight. She joined a health club, walked nine miles each week, and ate vegetables at all hours of the day. This plan succeeded for about four months, at which time she found new ways of getting fat. Karen ate celery, but the waterlogged vegetable tasted better with cheese and peanut butter smeared on top. Last August she ran out of fat-free dressing and started using a little of her husband's regular, promptly emptying the bottle in fifteen minutes.

Clearly a mental war wages for control of Karen's eating habits. It depresses this dieter to see her large rear end grow, so her mind repeatedly chooses the foods with the fewest calories, spending hours and even days plotting weight loss schemes, obsessing over every egg, each piece of kiwi fruit....

Unfortunately Karen's body came equipped with weapons of its own. Once her body loses weight, it alerts the stomach, the stomach relays messages to the mind. Every time her stomach growls Karen's mind takes notice. Each instance when the weight drops down slightly, the low grumbling intensifies. The mind fears the funny sounds and plots to overthrow the diet regime. Karen's mind fights valiantly for two actions that nearly exclude the possibility of each other, which are ending hunger, and achieving weight loss.

All of Karen's problems—a teenaged son, an unfaithful husband, and a stomach making too many decisions—leave her in a desperate condition. The stress-filled mental states she confronts, surely make you believe she is capable of lying to herself, with just the slightest nudge.

## Jim Conner II

Jim Conner, when not playing make-believe, is actually obsessed with the hostess named Mary at the large restaurant for which they both work. He likes the way she discreetly smiles at him when he walks past her station in the morning. Jim notices the slits in her dresses, black leather shoes, and long locks of blonde hair—basically everything about Mary. This lovestruck fool knows when the object of his affection goes to lunch, where she sits, what types of salads fill her plate, and how Mary plays with her carrots before putting them in her perfectly formed mouth.

Tragically, Mary's interests do not include Jim. She craftily selects her clothes to impress her boss not a busboy gawker, eats lunch at break time, dines in the rear of the restaurant away from the customers, picks salads that taste fresh, and still fondles her carrots neurotically the way she did when her mother hovered over her as a child. In other words, her thoughts include no Jim Connors.

Sadly the obsession continues despite the lack of interest on the part of the hostess. Love-struck Jim spends entire afternoons fantasizing about Mary loving him back, daydreaming of a meeting where Mary embraces him followed by hours of sexual indiscretion. His mind explores endless scenarios where Mary suddenly realizes his love fulfills her deep-seated need for romance and passion. Essentially tortured minds like Jim's consider every possibility of gaining an impossible lover's affection. He wants her so badly he dwells on the issue to the point of disrupting his work.

## Observation Number Three

The earlier, first group of illustrations established the existence of self-deception motives. The second group of observations, Jim's and Karen's, showed the lengths the mind travels in order to resolve a dilemma (lose sleep over an affair, wage war with itself over food, and pass days fantasizing about unattainable love). The third group of readily observable behaviors will demonstrate ways in which the mind tricks itself.

### Dreaming

Consider the case of the dreams filling the restful night. While sleeping, many wild ideas and bizarre visions fill the receptive mind and clearly fail the reality check. The events experienced during the quiet evenings never happen. Even if the dreamer sees them, feels them, and remembers them; the dreams resemble the actual world in only in a vague, confused way. Somehow the awake mind usually distinguishes which thoughts were real and which are imaginary, but in contrast, during many of these nocturnal fantasies, the person lying in bed cannot distinguish the fakes. And since the mind creates its own dreams, then you must conclude the mind betrays itself during the night. The mind just makes it up. (Clearly outside events influence the subject matter of dreams, but outside events are seldom the cause of nonsensical patterns of thought with limited connections to reality. [This book, of course, is one of the exceptions to the rule.])

## *Paul Jones*

The exaggeration of anxiety illustrates another example of mental fallacy. If Paul, a sophomore in college, suspects he may do poorly on an economics test, he sometimes starts worrying. Day after day the pressure builds as the exam date approaches. He loses sleep and finds more hair than usual in the bottom of the shower. Finally, by the time the big day arrives, Paul believes the fate of his entire college career rests on this one exam, but this assumption fails a common sense understanding. The questions only cover Paul's midterm knowledge for an elective class; the fate of his graduate school acceptance does not rest on a single exam, at least not this one. In reality Paul exaggerates and fools himself into thinking the list of questions have more importance than are justified, and since his mind controls the exaggerating; there is not a choice except to conclude once again that the mind misleads itself.

## Observation Number Four

Countless examples could be made, and others are made later, to illustrate just how widespread this type of doublethinking is. The questions that beg answering are: What limits or constrains the mind from fooling itself? When do we really start getting into trouble?

The fourth observation will answer some of the questions, that is solving the puzzle. It states that the mind will lie to itself if convinced dishonesty helps obtain the object desired. If the fourth observation holds, then many other questions arise, and these matters become a significant portion of this book.

To start with, consider the following: How does the mind go about trying to resolve problems via tricking itself? The first observation was that the people confront many conflicts and contradictions. The second observation was that people try hard to resolve them. Because of the extreme importance of some problems, attempts at resolving them create tension, and relieving that tension often takes on a life of its own. Too much mental activity trying to overcome a difficult dilemma makes the situation worse than having never tried in the first place. The third observation gave the mind another option: The mind possesses the ability of self-deception. It often finds more relief accepting a lie than anguishing without a solution; but using option three under duress profoundly affects everything. We only fool ourselves in attempts to solve problems.

## The Late Stanley Kaufman

A striking example of deception usually follows the death of a loved one. One of the mind's early reactions to death denies the passing away. We often want the loved one back so strongly we think almost anything is possible, and cannot acknowledge the obvious reality that death took a close friend or family member. The extreme nature of these emotions frees the mental processes to cheat in the most blatant way, rejecting the conspicuous termination of life.

We pretend uncle Stan still lives on the corner in the tan brick duplex. Stan walks out to get the newspaper each morning in his bare feet, while the garden continues to grow tall sweet corn, purple cabbage, and plump tomatoes; the lawn sprouts dandelions along with the occasional thistle. It seems as though nothing's changed with respect to Stan's state of being. We think about the times he greeted us with a big smile on Christmas carrying a bundle of presents, and the family picnic where he took on all his nephews and nieces in a game of softball. Everything is so vivid, indicating that all is well in our mind. Stan never left us, we just have to close our eyes for a moment to watch the movies playing inside our heads.

## Albert Fischer II

Another example reveals itself in the discussion of the afterlife. There are many objectives the mind wants very much but cannot have with respect to our own death. It desperately needs the answers and also wants a painless happy ending. If the existence of God could be determined with certainty, a large number of questions concerning death would be solved. We would have a goal in life of getting to heaven, and a purpose, to please the Lord. There would be order to the world, justice for all, and peace everlasting for the faithful. However some experiences might contradict God's being (like the acquaintances who are atheists) and lead a believer to doubting.

Since Albert wants to have a relationship with God, but isn't sure, he keeps trying to sort it out. The idea of a wonderful afterlife provides opportunity for affecting judgment, especially when compared to the possibility of a meaningless physical life followed by a hopeless ending. The divergent outcomes intensify the mental conflict, causing much worrying. For some (but not Albert) all the pressure can eventually lead to a false surrender to God and the denial of anything that contradicts his existence. Such a person may find peace at last in the warm glow of heavenly thoughts—but sugarcoating the notion of dying has nothing to do with the existence of God. The difficult thoughts about a fully terminating existence really only fool their minds into believing pleasant thoughts that may not be true.

## Albert Fischer III

On the opposite side of the issue lies another opportunity for deception. If Albert knows that his life is not consistent with God's commandments, it forces the consideration of other options. Thoughts of sex cause him to play mental games. Albert lusts for the beautiful woman he saw in a movie, fantasizing about her sad eyes, her legs, her smile…. (Obviously an actress cannot reciprocate the lust of each one of her millions of fans. Therefore, short of kidnapping her, Albert must make do with photographs and movies.) Originally Albert enjoyed making love with the woman he married and focused his attention there. Many years later however, his wife (the actual sex mate) gained a few pounds and lost Albert's true affection. So when Albert has intercourse with his wife of twenty-three years, he substitutes an actress vision, thereby removing the stale memory that lies physically beneath him. Creating the illicit fantasies alleviates his sexual cravings, particularly his lust for the actress.

How does sex relate to God? Does the Bible make it okay to act like Albert? No! Albert must deny the teachings of Christ to free his conscience, to enjoy the moment. He must press the mute button to stop the warning sirens in his head. Albert must act as If there is no God to reach the highest climax during sex.

## John Zatti

Addictive behaviors bring out the worst sort of doublethinking. John passes through the liquor store door to purchase his second bottle of gin for the day. Feeling the anguish of a life filled with lying and misdeeds, his actions are slowly destroying the emotional stability of his wife and children. The drunken dad knows he must stop binging in order to turn his life around—and so the father of four, on a whim, decides to quit. But today is Saturday, so he plans to party one more night, and tomorrow make up to the old lady as well as the kids. John even intends to return to the *group* and get things fixed, well… tomorrow—or so John has deceived himself.

How does John distort his perspective on the cruelty inflicted so blatantly on the little girls and their mother? Everyone around him can see through his immaturity. His poor spouse endures the hangovers and begs him to quit. John promised giving up the liquor several times, and he usually believed it. His children shudder with fear during his violent mood swings, and the drunken bum even knows for himself that the time to renounce alcohol once and for all is long overdo. But not tonight.

John's supervisor at the packinghouse fired him two months ago, but he couldn't stand the bitch anyway. He borrowed money from a close drinking buddy—the fourth time this month—planning to pay back the loan when he gets a job. (Clearly John's self-deception inflicts pain and suffering on himself as well as those around him. Generally speaking, deception associates with all that defines wickedness and evil. That affiliation unfortunately, is the burden that doublethink the philosophy will need to overcome.)

## Altogether

Using deception in these ways leads to very peculiar situations. Resolution by lying to oneself usually fixes no problems; in effect it often only prolongs the predicament, sometimes making it much worse. A difficulty arises and proves hard to solve so a person chooses a lie, but sooner or later the consequences of corruption take their toll; philosophies stop making sense; life becomes confused; chaos reigns.

If you accept the fourth observation—about lying to ourselves to gain an objective—then everything valued in life comes under scrutiny. How can a woman determine if her mind actually desires something, or if it simply bluffed itself into believing it needs an object to obtain another it wants, or thinks it wants even more? Perhaps at the base of a person's morals lies a set of fundamental values. These principles might represent spiritual and/or physical reality. They could however become convoluted in an attempt to obtain other incompatibly wished-for ends. The mind may manipulate itself into changing the base rules it considers absolute. In other words, there may be no way to ever find what guides us from the center of our being.

If the mind proves capable of deceiving itself, and the motives are strong, what limits the falseness? What prevents the mind from directing the person it controls to murder, rape, steal, abuse, lie, and cheat? What stops us from committing all these sorts of evil acts? I would presume if reasonable fundamental basic guidelines controlled our thoughts, these crimes and sins would never occur, but yet they happen all the time. People commit the brutal offenses either strictly because no basic barrier exists in the mind or the mind in these cases deceives itself into ignoring the rules, or the combination of the mind lying and other external factors causes it to commit the opposite of what it fundamentally values.

## The Solution

There are many ways to resolve a problem that do not make any sense. The temptations to fool oneself seem great indeed. Personal integrity eludes the most diligent thinker. But understanding doublethink changes that. The intentional doublethinker becomes the expert of corruption and knows where the lies hide, what they look like, how they are used, and how to extinguish the ones causing harm. Doublethinking becomes a tool that seeks out manipulation before crushing it. Doublethinking creates a new set of nonsense, and then something changes; it cures the mind's problems in a manner we can only partially understand.

# 3 Logic and Illogic:
## Understanding a World with Both

*...oh dear, how puzzling it all is! I'll try if I know all the things I used to know. Let me see: four times five is twelve, and four times six is thirteen, and four times seven is—oh dear! I shall never get to twenty at that rate!*
—LEWIS CARROLL, *ALICE'S ADVENTURES IN WONDERLAND*

Chapter one stated, "Doublethink breaks down logic." But does that make any sense? Is it even possible? Can something seem so solid, and then just fall apart? What fills the void left by ending sensible reasoning? Does everything reduce to mindless rambling? Few ever question logic, but what if rationality abandoned us, or it was always misused? Is the world just a bucket of gibberish? Would that matter? Would anyone recognize the difference? What standard judges mumbo jumbo in the universe of babbling?

Whether logic is broken down or not gets considered soon enough, but first we will examine the meaning of *logic*. Dictionaries describe logic as "the science of correct reasoning." This definition serves no purpose for this book, since it assumes a correct form of reasoning exists. Furthermore it implies that using the 'correct' method of thinking is a good thing. Instead, it is easier to simply explain how logic works. Starting with two pieces of information, logic creates a new one. For example, assume the following two statements are true:

All cats hate all dogs.
Spot is a dog.

Taking into account this knowledge, the rules of logic create a new fact:

All cats hate Spot.

Logical statements of the type shown above gain acceptance from almost everyone. (Expert logicians follow similar patterns and of course use more sophistication.)

But what about other kinds of arguments? A doublethinker believes that all cats love Spot, or that the third statement is false. One cannot prove that the mind works only a certain way, so choose from the many possibilities. Simply state that the third is true, false, and somewhere in-between; or just say the answer proves irrelevant and nonexistent. Declare that the first and second statements are true in the ordinary sense, and also are not true and also are nonexistent. Why not agree that the third seems false, and that even though first and second are true? It really no longer matters.

Traditional logic cannot escape reproach. Our minds do not have to behave a certain way. Nobody set the rules governing reasoning into place for all eternity. Play with logic, manipulate your brain, exercise freedom of thought, and make rational anything at all. Chapter two proved the possibility of doing exactly that.

Up goes down. Down flows up. Inside thinks outside. Good looks bad. Bad shoots geese. Back went forth while forth leftover. All fish walk and stay the same. Whatever works, works, and whatever confuses, confuses. Nothing feels real as everything appears imagined. Black looks good and gray tastes white. What leaves here stays put. When it stops making sense, it starts making truth.

## Why?

Many readers again find this sort of nonsense nauseating. Unfortunately, even vomiting fails to make the case for traditional logic; wanting common sense to prevail will not force it to—no matter how much doublethink twitches and turns our innards. Choosing doublethink to go away is not a deciding factor in determining whether doublethink disappears.

Perhaps the key to understanding logic then comes form revealing why we value constancy in some cases and why foolishness gains acceptance in other cases. What makes an individual select logic or illogic? Normal reasoning cannot be proven the only choice or possibility. Logic could be coherent or it could be doublethink. In some instances however we prefer traditional logic to silliness and doublethink. In these cases, since no reasoning justifies selecting sense over nonsense, those who chose the ordinarily intelligent approach obviously tricked themselves into believing that it was somehow better than the alternative.

A business traveler, for instance, drives to an airport. He picked this particular airport according to where he lives. He reasoned that if he drove to San Francisco to save airfare, it would take much more of his valuable time than the added cost of the ticket warrants. He also believes flying provides the safest form of travel. He used logical thinking in the traditional sense in a practical and careful manner. It saves money and makes him happy. Why would such a sensible man ever question logic?

In chapter two a mental model was presented that demonstrates how motives in general can deceive. The following repeats from chapter two:

1. There exist many desires that are difficult to obtain and cannot be fulfilled.
2. We sometimes become desperate.
3. The mind possesses the ability to deceive itself.
4. The mind will deceive itself if convinced dishonesty helps obtain the object desired.

The above model provides a very simplified mechanism for the business traveler to bias his thoughts toward logic over illogic. One unattainable desire is that of most businessmen: He wants significantly more money than he can have. He works seventy hours a week, demonstrating that he tries desperately to obtain wealth. Meanwhile he dreams of joining the likes of Bill Gates and Warren Buffet, even though that will never happen. Thus his actions confirm an ability to dupe himself.

From watching other businessmen succeed he notices a pattern: Using logic improves the bottom line. He then thinks the best of logic, since it leads to more money, and in general agrees with his own personal experiences. Furthermore, reflecting on the past reminds him that sensibility served him well, and he concludes confidently that reasoning is good.

Perhaps few find fault with the end result of accepting logic as beneficial for a traveling businessperson, but what does it mean if the businessman accepts traditional rationalizations due to self-deception? What if the explanation for the use and existence of reasoning relies on a mental trick or an incomplete understanding? No proof exists for thinking logic is correct; so if a man feels coherent thinking is right, he does so for something other than a desire for consistency.

What prevents the business traveler from finding that coherent thought is bad? What if the business traveler later observed that stealing and other law breaking lead to greater wealth? What if the business traveler gathered his or her peers were having sex with their secretaries and receiving immense pleasure? What if he discovered illegal drugs enhanced performance in the business world?

Eventually these "logically" chosen acts would cause his demise. The sensible, rational, loving businessman would become a drug-addicted imprisoned divorcee. At that point, he would conclude from the circumstances that logic is bad. Logic told him if others could cheat on their taxes and wives, then he could as well. But the likely resulting change in lifestyle would make him skeptical. Clearly the path to solving the problem of logic could go in virtually any direction.

## Foundations

But many logic believers also maintain that to make sense, the world needs a solid foundation with ties into values, otherwise the goals always confuse and complicate. Furthermore, selecting the alternative only suggests mindlessness, circular reasoning, and just plain evil.

The doublethink philosophy believes a completely consistent world *does* need a solid basis but a doublethink world doesn't. Doublethink allows any sort of beginning. Nothing really makes sense, so why not say anything at all? Just pick the truth and be done with the matter; it won't make any sense, and it won't have to. How much better could life be making anything you authenticate right and wrong? A person just decides the foundation and builds from there—or lays the footings to construct elsewhere. If the building tips over, just change it; start again; make the rules a little better. Nobody can sort out the absurdity so anything can be. Pick whatever rules make sense: Make life unbearable; choose the opposite of sanity; think the opposite of thought; or do nothing at all. Everything and anything goes—or nothing goes.

The mind values both logic and illogic. The mind accepts either completely when sufficiently motivated. The mind uses the ability of self-deceiving to embrace the existence and consequences of coherence and corruption. The mind follows either sense or nonsense when the incentives are strong. The evidence proves the human mind practices both normal and abnormal reasoning.

## Flip a Coin

At this point many are irritated and tempted to ignore all my malarkey and simply accept logic. The minds of the impatient readers can use the motivation of avoiding doublethink to obtain a form of consistent reasoning. Obviously some resentment follows from not knowing whether truth exists, and certainly simple honest proofs assist people in making decisions about right and wrong. Therefore whether or not logic's derivation consists of legitimate and infallible techniques matters little, since people do have a strong motive to want logic. And when they have a strong motive to believe in correct thoughts they can easily lie to themselves and accept that course of action.

Now consider this specific example of an assumption generally believed to be true: Two plus eight equals ten. But is it true for certain or is there a motive for wanting it to be true? In the real world math could be completely wrong. For instance:

> Two cars pull into an empty lot and park; ten minutes later eight more cars do the same. The parking attendant saw this happen. His boss calls him on the phone to ask how many cars entered the lot. The attendant tells him "five." Why shouldn't he answer five? His suspicious boss checks the parking spaces, counting ten cars. The boss gets mad. The attendant then refutes his employer's methods of adding and now claims there are just two cars in the lot. As would be expected the attendant is fired, providing him with a financial motive for wanting to follow regular math on his next job. But just because the math-challenged man applies for government benefits the following week, weird counting does not make

him wrong. Why must there be ten cars in the lot? There really does not have to be any particular number. There are seven, twenty, one thousand, and zero cars lined up in neat rows. Like all mental processes, math does not need to rely on certain rules.

If everyone acted like the attendant, then much of the world would fall apart. Banks would not operate because the tellers would hand out and take in money in nonsensical ways. Carpenters would build heaps of lumber and piles of brick instead of houses. Schoolteachers would teach nonsense but really would not need to since nonsense is very easily learned. Incompetent farmers would grow weeds instead of wheat. The bakers may not notice since they no longer produced bread anyway. Ultimately the entire population of the world would risk starvation.

But if all of those conditions occurred it still does not prove that adding numbers in the normal method demonstrates an example of a true assumption. Those same conditions, however, indicate that strong motivation exists for wanting math and logic in the traditional way. But once again, wishing something true does not, in fact, make it the only path to follow. The world is the way it is—not the way the mathematicians want it to be.

Many hold a belief in the desirability of consistent and repeatable patterns of expressing and manipulating numbers, and these individuals refuse to count like the attendant. For example, it seems unlikely that young married couples will start hiring carpenters that dispute the basic principles of math and measuring, but still, you cannot prove math has to only be a certain way. Algebra and arithmetic consist of a fantasy, a mental place someone can go to visit, providing comfort, perhaps, just knowing that such a location exists.

It may seem that logic, in the traditional sense, receives value by expanding knowledge. Many contend knowledge creates power, increases wealth, and avoids dangerous situations. Information combined with logic allows more depth in understanding and gives security. Reasoning provides a foundation for better living and also a building block for science.

A doublethink advocate would simply say that these traits of logic only indicate even more motives for wanting algebra and arithmetic the normal way. Logic's meaning in an absolute sense is abstract. Abstract means to separate. Logic separates from the real world. Reason applied to life compares to Soren Kierkegaard's 'leap of faith.' Living proves no connection unless the mind assumes one. Just like a belief in God, a solid foundation for thinking consistently eludes us.

Furthermore, the premise of using logic to gain its benefits presents a serious threat to the followers of the craft, since the justification applies to the inverse as well. Illogic also gives comfort, creates wealth, provides benefits, and adds value; in addition its absurdities are also abstracted from life. One could have a 'leap of faith' for irrationality as easily as for rationality. Some would prefer that the truth battle falseness and destroy it, but the examination of life exposes the existence of incorrect reasoning, and in the war for gaining control of our minds, no victor emerges. Thus, silliness and sanity must coexist.

Perhaps it feels awkward to live in such a world where logic could cause suffering, but consider a trial where the prosecutor tries to convince a jury you shot your next-door neighbor by stating the following:

"You admit being at the scene of the crime and had a motive. Your gun, along with your bullets, shot the victim. Your fingerprints were on the trigger, and finally six witnesses claim they saw you shoot and scream *'die pig!'*"

Damn logic! But fear not; simply hire an attorney to convince a jury the most improper reasoning applies in your case. Your defense team might present arguments that sound remarkably similar to those used to argue intelligently. Your admitting to being at the scene of the crime proves nothing, since your rights were not explained to you—besides, you live at the scene. You thought your neighbor feminine, but he dated many women and no men. Your sexual orientation confused your motive. Furthermore the trial covers murder, not your right to own a handgun. Fingerprints on the trigger were planted there by the actual murderer, and the five witnesses misunderstood your screaming about the pet pig you wanted to butcher. And finally, you did not consider the victim pig-like, really more of a jerk. (The strategy is to toss common sense out the window, simply muddling the jury until an emotional appeal gains sympathy.)

A lawyer's job often pays well for polluted reasoning. Defenders promote the interests of their clients, not some abstract right and wrong, truth and justice baloney. Do attorneys refuse cases where their client clearly committed homicide? Rest assured that regardless of how obvious the guilt and horrendous the crime, a defender awaits to plead your cause to keep you out of jail. A hired doublethinker pledges a sacred oath to integrity and morality; he earns his keep by twisting, bending, and breaking all reason as well as rationale to convince twelve peers of your innocence.

Who would you trust even less than a lawyer? How about the guy who greets you when you are looking for a used car? Is he forbidden from lying? No, because some information interferes with making the deal. If a salesman knows a potential customer needed a minivan but does not have one in his lot, he can instead subtly suggest a two-seated Corvette, explaining all the features of a lightweight roadster. He should ignore its utter impracticality to a man with five children. The unscrupulous con artist does not rely on legitimate reasons to sell a vehicle to a person ill suited for a sports car. It would be crazy to do otherwise, at least in his mind.

What if you started a company? Perhaps your company's potential looks bleak. The ideal people to have invest in this sham include the extremely wealthy. You may also seek those who enjoy throwing their money into suspicious schemes that will most likely fail. It is really too bad that many such dolts have already gone broke, investing in opportunities similar to yours. Since starting an enterprise without capital proves difficult, you decide to try illogic. You emphasize the huge potential payback of e.gizmos.com and fail to mention that the likelihood of bankruptcy approaches ninety-nine percent. Skip over the negative return rate on the earlier investors' money, while portraying the e-business format that you intend to use as revolutionary, when in fact it is easily copied and unpatentable. Claim your runaway best-selling green gizmo makes a radical departure from the old way, while ignoring that thirty others already started e-businesses using nearly identical technology selling light green and blue gizmos. In order to make the transaction happen and obtain the working capital, use corrupted pleas, convincing morons to invest in your sham, a near certain failure and financial abyss.

Gateway computer salespeople have times when their latest version unquestionably underperforms and breaks more often than a Dell. Does that stop them from peddling a Gateway? Usually not. They still make an effort to tout their Office 200X features even when the customer is better served by the reliability of Office 200X running on a Dell. Gateway keeps putting up pictures of black and white cows and continues to boast of the most giga-something or other.

Often the customer may even get further ahead buying nothing at all. Perhaps the customer has been brainwashed by television commercials showing toddlers typing in front of phonics and shape recognition games. Without consulting a child psychologist, he heads straight for the Gateway retail store on Junior's second birthday to purchase the most powerful system in the brochure. Using ordinary rational thinking in this instance would mean the customer left empty-handed, but the unsympathetic salesman will no doubt earn a healthy commission pandering to the customer's media-controlled whims. This lucky salesman need never doubt the value of ill reasoning.

How many other cases of desirable deception exist? If it is good some of the time, then why not all of the time? Are logic and illogic value neutral? Or just mixed? Consider another case for nonsense by trying a new assumption: Hypothesize a consistent system that really works. Theorize a logical method that is either subjectively true or objectively true, and this pattern of thought runs into difficulty too. It fails to explain what to do with the untrue. Illogic also exists, is unavoidable, and often proves undetectable. Even though illogic tolerates logic, the inverse does not follow. Logic despises the ways of illogic. A comprehensive and consistent method is not a robust approach. A little mistake here and there completely messes up everything.

The Catholic Church of Martin Luther's time had a strict hierarchy. In essence the Church never erred. With everything moving along fairly smoothly during the end of the Middle Ages, Martin Luther pointed out obvious flaws and contradictions. His accusations against Rome and the Holy Father shattered the Catholic Church's utter dominance of western Europe. Protesting the paying of money for the forgiving of sins forced the leadership to make the little-known monk into a famous heretic.

One of the keys to unraveling the monopoly of Catholicism arose from exposing illogical activities clearly inconsistent with the Bible and Christ's teachings. Quite simply, the Church contradicted the Bible. Indeed it seemed unlikely to many that the Church (or Popes) failed, but mistakes happened. So incompatible with this sort of 'illogic' was the Church, that it took five hundred years for the first Pope to admit that God's grace ascends a soul to heaven, not man's deeds.

Even today a tremendous logic based fear prevents the Church's authority from unwinding within (except by those willing to become subjects of excommunication). One of the main thrusts of the Catholic dogma includes the simple bit of reasoning for the descending rule from Christ to Peter to all the popes. But this little chunk of logic needs only one misguided soul or humble fanatic with protests and demonstrations of evil at the top to throw the whole church into turmoil.

Another problem with logic comes from rigidly carrying the practice to the extreme and causing insanity. Suppose a person valued consistency, while also placing high value on several other things like sex and money. What if it turned out that the ideals the person sought out were not compatible? What if that individual believed strongly in a system of values that did not add up? In certain circumstances, reasoning turns awful, helping to explain how people can and do go insane.

Personal computers are extreme examples of logical devices, frequently crashing when the internal critical flip-flops become inconsistent. Attempting to divide by zero or conducting an infinite do-loop are reminders of the computer's rational limitations. Locking up and scrambling characters confound users on a regular basis. Many times the computer would better serve its user by simply ignoring the little glitch and moving on, but often it cannot do so because the internal circuits and software are not tolerant of miscalculations.

Luckily, unlike computers, most humans seem to have the ability to reprogram to circumvent inconsistencies. Humans allow themselves a wrong function; when all else fails, ignore what you know to be right. Deceive yourself if sufficient cause justifies fraud, simply accepting lies if the results appear less painful than strict adherence to a path leading to certain insanity.

(Sadly the system is not perfect; the wrong function does not always arrive when needed. Some people still get caught up in series of repetitive patterns of behavior. A woman rationalizes, for example, that germs are bad. She washes her hands to make sure they are clean. She scrubs them again to be extra sure. Germs cause disease so she does it once more. You cannot be too certain so she turns on the faucet rubs the bar of soap between her hands….

A new false assumption provides one way of breaking down this pattern. Perhaps she need only convince herself that germs are good, or that washing too often encourages bacteria growth. Silly behavior escapes logical traps and forms patterns of actions bounded by new thinking. Corrupted thought patterns allow consideration of ideas that pure logical reasoning would rule out of consideration. Not that washing your hands compulsively demonstrates sensible logic; the act is, however, bound by logic. The rules, the structure, and the discipline needed to carry out such a foolish chain of events all suggest a strict system infiltrated by a bit of stupidity. Adding more mixed-up thoughts like that of intentional doublethink merely allows the pattern to break loose easier than going back and finding the original flawed thought. Logical systems are not directly tied to life; rather they imply a nonexistent objective or subjective truth exists, but it is simply not there.)

## Build Anyway

Look at true and false from another perspective. Without denying the world's nonsense and lack of coherence, it might help to approach the art of thinking from a different direction. Assuming for a moment that only traditional logic has a point, or makes sense, there still exist a number of problems with the application of regular logic to the practical world.

One of the biggest problems is the possibility of no valid assumptions, no certain theories, no absolute proofs, no meaningful arguments, and so forth; not one single true assumption or statement existing. Perhaps no bit of self-evident reasoning finds its way into the human mind. The world is the way it is, or it isn't the way it is, but no propositions remain on which to build. Nothing prevails for certain. Logic needs a bottom from which to rise, but if nothing proves true, then logic gets stopped at its foundation. (Illogic could fill the gap. If offered the opportunity, creative imaginations can provide the necessary givens allowing reason to function.)

Theoretically speaking, how does a person discover a truth? What is known and never disputed? Epistemology studies the ability to know or what can be known. Western philosophers have been arguing about this subject since at least Pyrrho, and after considerable, extended debate over knowing and how to know, little agreement has resulted. Some make the case for only the existence of subjective knowledge based on sensory information. Others battle for the existence of objective truths but limited means for man grasping them, saying sensory information is incomplete and misleading, believing that true knowledge comes from outside the mind. This debate literally never ends. (I won't bore you with the details; take my word for it—they are endless.) Since so many others have argued the subject without reaching a consensus, suffice it to say that the controversy of epistemology makes doublethink appear to be the only practical choice. In other words, when there is no solution to this problem that dates to at least ancient Greece, there is only doublethink.

For the sake of argument, assume that logic is good in and of itself. Then assume there are facts to be said about the real world that are beyond dispute. Philosophers demonstrate just such behavior when making statements about the real world—or at least they claim to. They use logic in very interesting ways; when it suits the ideas the philosopher believes, reason is good and fine. When reason does not adequately explain a situation, they toss it aside.

Metaphysics, divine mysteries, and existentialism help fill in the weaker points of logic. Various forms of metaphysics have explained the facets of the flat world and how the sun travels around the earth. Divine mysteries are those confusions that two thousand years of Christianity have failed to sort out (like how God is three beings and still just one). Existentialism is merely an admission of how hard the task of philosophy is, without capitulating completely to doublethink. Philosophy is filled with bad logic to get through the difficult situations; these are just three of the common techniques.

A preacher provides a good example of a typical philosopher. When a preacher wants to bring nonbelievers to God, he doesn't always make sound, consistent, reasonable arguments. Instead he can rely on a feeling of a divine presence unbounded by an earthly understanding of the world. He may emphasize God's love, forgiveness, and generosity (or create fear with threats of eternal damnation). He has an indirect way of saying that religion needs no logic, and no amount of thinking explains salvation. Instead the evangelist can rely on bliss, fear, love, and intimidation to lead the follower to God.

By the same token, this sort of manipulation does not prevent the ordained shepherd from using and misusing logic to gather as well as control his sheep. Since the time of Jesus, church leaders of all Christian faiths have taken words like 'true' and 'false,' and then packed them with ideas only loosely tied to logic. "God is truth. Truth is good. Injustice is false. The devil is false. False is bad." These extra slippery bits of logic make little sense, because all these ideas are independent of each other and cannot be tied together consistently except when using extreme care.

What happens when the devil speaks the truth to gain the trust of the faithful? Would a parent not celebrate a false positive cancer test report on their four-year-old son? What prevents me from making false statements about God's lustful aspirations?

Religious advocates are certainly not alone in the abuse of logic. Karl Marx and Frederick Engels's *Communist Manifesto* logically explains as well as documents the tyranny of the wealthy over the poor. Perhaps they should have stopped there, but instead they went on to proclaim the need for violent revolution to end the oppression.

*Let the ruling classes tremble at a communist revolution. The proletarians have nothing to lose but their chains. They have the world to win. Workingmen of all countries. Unite!*

—KARL MARX AND FREDERICK ENGELS [1848] 1955

The only solution acceptable to a communist was the complete destruction of capitalism. It is ironic that in the long run the capitalists did not require an overthrow, just time to improve technology and free enterprise to the point where the workers of the world fled communism, not the money-grubbing tycoons. No doubt the threat of communist revolution tempered the wealthy pigs, but it was these pigs who eventually created the powerful economic systems (with limited socialism) that undermined the fanatical altruists.

And what about democracy? Thomas Jefferson wrote (with the help of others) the Declaration of Independence, which holds certain "truths to be self-evident." What is a "self-evident truth"? Are Jeffersonian ideals so obvious they can never be refuted? And if they are so simple to comprehend, then why is it necessary to fight to protect them? Aren't they as apparent to others as they are to Americans?

There is another method of considering the merit of these famous political figures along with the religious ones. Think about the possibility that the evangelists, Jefferson, Marx, and Engels were all doublethinkers—free to express mere ideas as truth. Who could blame them? Where else are you going to find your core beliefs if you can't just make them up? Does morality derive truth fundamentally from nothing? If it can't be determined fundamentally, then why isn't it acceptable to just jump in anywhere?

Philosophers since the beginning of civilization (probably sooner) simply pulled truths out of the air, including Socrates and Plato, as well as Nietzsche and Freud; they just made wild-ass guesses and proceeded with their work. No sensible people accept completely the philosophy of any of the so-called great thinkers (with the occasional exception of religious fundamentalists). Regardless, all the well-known philosophers were saying things they could not support logically and consistently, and yet these men were the bright ones, the geniuses. How much hope does the average person have if the *best* can't make any sense?

Logic cannot be proven to exist. Without logic the world lapses into confusion filled with doublethink. Doublethink allows for anything and everything. Consequently, a person could make logic exist, and by the same token a person could make logic not exist. But if reason finds a place in the world, doublethink doesn't just disappear, and if doublethink really does exist, a person might choose to have common sense not exist. Therefore, logic does not exist. Therefore, logic exists.

Getting back to normal logic, another consequence arises to keep in mind—the opportunity to go on stating truths. Since there are no fundamentals to compare them to, any proposition can be truth. Whatever is stated is correct. Everything makes sense and confusion disappears. Although nothing has meaning without a solid base, everything has meaning too, keeping all explanations of the world valid, and everything about the universe real, true, fair, and good.

# 4 Empiricism:
## Considering the Other Options

*If I claim to be a wise man, it surely*
*means that I don't know.*
—KANSAS, "CARRY ON MY WAYWARD SON"

Without repudiating the world's nonsense, it might help to examine reasoning from yet another perspective, allowing for the possibility that some facts are known for certain; that is, some axioms are assured true. Leave the door open to the possibility the mind can build on this thought process to solve the doublethink dilemma. Maybe a world exists to make sense of. Per chance, a group of suppositions when carefully handled, unravel such problems as abortion or homosexuality, or even find a better way to answer to questions about God's existence.

Where to begin? What demonstrates absolute certainty? Seemingly the only concepts known beyond a doubt are from the method of trial and error, or empiricism. (Subjectivity leaves everything else open to disagreement.) Assuming that to be the case, empirical methods might provide hope for building a true model of the world—and this model might resolve the confusion.

Empiricism parallels logic, gaining acceptance without question (unless conflicting with another belief, such as a religious one). But what is empiricism? Roughly put, empiricism rings a bell when considering jumping off the side of the Grand Canyon. The person peering over the edge hears the dinging in his ear to help to remind him that almost every time someone leaps from the side of a huge crack in the earth they die. In general empiricism tells us not to attempt stunts like wingless flight unless we want to splatter ourselves on the banks of the Colorado River. Stated more precisely, empiricism dictates what we see happen a thousand times before in the identical set of circumstances, we see again the one thousandth and first time as well.

Admittedly the concept of empiricism seems to have potential. Imagine an empirical world view built piece by piece, refined over thousands of years by countless individuals improving the human lot, only accepting what works and always reserving the right to check the answer by testing to see if the expected events repeat. It seems quite reasonable and is a part of the scientific method.

But why trust empericism? Must things continue on the same path as before? Could I not assume that the next person who hops off the Grand Canyon lands on both feet and walks away? What fundamentally makes canyon jumping dangerous? (By the way, I recommend other means of disproving empiricism.) Why believe the things that transpired yesterday forecast tomorrow? Is the human mind obligated to assume that it must follow the normal course of action anyway? Why not plan for the sun to rise in the west on Thursday? Claim that a river will start flowing up the side of a mountain. Why not suppose any sort of nonsense at all?

What justifies empiricism? If a person thinks his or her thoughts in an empirical manner and wants to know why, it doesn't make any sense. The word *why* asks an empirical question. How is it possible for there to be reasons for reasons to exist? And if there were no reasons for reasons, why have reasons? Or are there simply causes without cause? Do scientific proofs pop up like mushrooms with nothing in particular to back them up? Can anyone just imagine them, or must they arrive from some place far away and mysterious? Are humans not free to believe in anything?

Clearly not all people embrace empiricism; in fact, many show evidence of flat out denying it. Casinos succeed because gamblers willingly bet hoping to defy the odds, many wagering over and over, fully aware that the more bets placed, the more money the house wins. They seemingly never wonder where all the money comes from for casinos to decorate so lavishly and pay for the commercials on TV.

In a similar vein, some young drivers attempt to break the laws of physics, navigating corners at excessive speeds, while ignoring centrifugal forces. These silly teenage racers hope to prove Isaac Newton wrong, ignoring warnings from textbooks, friends, teachers, and parents—many young drivers prefer danger. They skip careful calculations of the maximum speed and angles needed for surviving a curve in the road, preferring to propel their steel and rubber rockets with a gut feeling accompanied by a sense of danger. Often alcohol inspires the added confidence needed to make their fateful decisions.

Other kinds of anti-empiricists believe in psychic powers and witchcraft. These superstitious idiots sometimes believe Friday the thirteenth and black cats bring bad luck—but who proves them wrong when they can only be mistaken if empiricism proves right. Yet nobody's done that!

## Try Another Approach

Although not accepting the world makes sense, give empiricism the benefit of the doubt and it runs into the same trouble that logic finds in the application to real cases. Who ever knows with absolute certainty that an observed event repeats in the identical situation, with all the relevant variables falling into place as before, and therefore empiricism reliably predicts the outcome? Name one individual that prognosticates while taking all possible factors under consideration.

This obsession may seem a little picky, but what if eternal life revolved around a bit of knowledge? What if your own personal investigation made you ninety-five percent confident there was no god, with only a few little questions remaining open? Who accepts ninety-five percent odds if it means a five percent possibility of spending eternity in hell? How far do you trust empiricism? To eternity?

To the other extreme, empiricism (just like logic) takes exceptional abuse from the religious community, applying well and good, until contradicting the Bible; then the faithful simply abandon common sense. What kind of empirical person believes the Bible's description of the creation of the world, instead of looking at the rocks to see the overwhelming evidence of evolution? Fossils combined with isotope dating explain all kinds of interesting facts about ancient and prehistoric times—unfortunately the techniques also contradict God's word, therefore cause and effect are set aside by those who want to believe.

Even though fundamentalist Christians scoff at notions like the survival of the fittest when the discussion covers monkeys and Charles Darwin, but this doesn't mean a devoted Christian cannot accept or enjoy the modern results of centuries of empirical investigation. Without guilt of any sort, a devout Christian can ride in jet aircraft, drink pasteurized milk, own super computers, and receive flu immunizations; taking advantage of a world improved by scientists proves trivial for the religious fundamentalist. He need only separate a biologist's Darwinian beliefs from the germ-free irradiated hamburger in his fridge. Call one heresy and the other a delicious lunch.

In the New Testament it is written that Jesus died, then rose from the dead on the third day. No reasonable explanation accounts for Jesus's reincarnation—yet hundreds of millions of people live by this "biblical fact." The Old Testament also tells of Moses parting the Red Sea but provides no physics theory for that happening either. Christians—and Jews—often accept the scriptures literally, but fall under no obligation to badmouth the desirable results of the trial-and-error method.

As a doublethinker, the Christian can accept both as truth, or neither, or some of each, or whatever. As a proud member of the community, he or she may legitimately adopt the position of a God-fearing scientist. His or her tossed-salad logic fully confirms that everything read in the Bible promotes nonsense worth living for.

## Another Perspective

The philosophical side of extreme empiricism presents another significant problem. The empirical zealot might conclude that under a given set of circumstances another set of conditions necessarily follow. Furthermore, if all the exact states of our world could be known, then it would be possible to predict all the events in this realm. If this were the case, then all circumstances in our corner of the universe would drop into place, or more commonly stated, "this world would be determined."

But maybe the world is undetermined. What links empiricism to determinism? Somebody observed an event and also noticed a set of circumstances proceeds that event for each occurrence; this allowed others to extrapolate that all events have preceding causes.

I, on the other hand, have personal knowledge that this is not so. I personally was too busy writing this book and observed no reason for the war in Kosovo. Later I also noticed many other events in the newspaper occurred without events leading up to them. I, therefore, extrapolated stories in the newspaper are beyond the reach of empiricism, and after making this extrapolation I have been pleasantly surprised by daily confirmations of the unpredicted articles filling the paper. In fact, if empiricism were the full explanation of the world, I could forecast tomorrow's news and stop paying for my newspaper subscription. In other words, saying the world is determined does not make the entire world predictable or even remotely so.

But how well does empiricism prognosticate the everyday world? When turning right at an intersection, traffic law dictates the use of a turn signal, since empirical knowledge does not reliably tell us which way another car will go. Or to put it in terms of prediction, much of the world remains unpredictable. The unstated premise of determinism implies everything is potentially foreseeable; therefore, the events of the world are known in advance. Unfortunately, this demonstrates yet another misguided "leap of faith."

But just in case I am wrong and the determinists are on to something, assume they are correctly assessing the situation. What, then, does determinism really mean? Perhaps the phrase "cause and effect" better explains the concept. An event occurred prior to another event, so we say the former caused the latter. But why? You should also go back another step and consider the episode that caused the earlier one the root event. Then extrapolate that a chain of events all had prior causes that were also events. In essence, all causes are previous events and all events are causes for future events.

Unfortunately for the believer, this undercuts the role of God. Why does God cause a world with people in it and then subject them to the physical laws of his choosing, while reserving the option of condemning them to hell for their bad behavior? Would judgment day consist of an all-powerful God judging his own works? Of course not, but God makes no sense if everything down to the way we comb our hair and who we choose to sleep with is determined. In addition, he may be thinking our thoughts and causing every action through his control of the very laws of physics he created in the beginning of time.

So let us cut to the chase. There really are just four viable solutions to this problem:

1. Empiricism/determinism is valid, but there is no God.
2. There is a doublethinking God.
3. Cause and effect is not universal; in other words, some effects lack causes.
4. Doublethinking is valid.

Starting with item one, you could ignore the philosophical dilemma, and just learn to accept a life where there is no God. Then if empiricism is the case, the world is sterile and predictable, but it is what it is. There is no reason to judge what is predetermined by an omnipotent being.

Or you could chose item two or four, which really means accepting one of the many forms of doublethink. Cause and effect's relationship to God—who cares?

Finally you could choose item three, which undercuts empiricism since it becomes impossible to know what events were caused and which were without cause. In other words for item three, empiricism equals yet another type of doublethink, sometimes it applies and other times it fails.

Therefore, we must admit either there is no God, empiricism is not universal, or there is doublethink. But even assuming item one is the only path left for maintaining consistency in reason, it does not follow that atheists never doublethink.

# Nietzsche

Stipulate that God is dead, as Nietzsche did, and a fully empirical outlook provides a way to view the world even many atheists detest (Nietzsche [1882] 2001, 3.108). Determinism seemingly says to many that actions taken cannot affect the world. Our very being is the way it is and men and women are hopelessly obeying fate, living out pathetic existences, all of which were set in place at the beginning of time during the big bang. Nothing matters; there is no such thing as crime; human actions are caused, so we need hold no people accountable for their deeds, as they were all preordained.

But you might notice that a deterministic world view flows from a prediction based on observation, while observation demonstrates human behavior relies on mental activity. Even when one acknowledges this empirically derived fact, it still frightens many to the point of hating determinism. They rebel against the notion that a predetermined world means all thinking changes nothing, assuming that everyone would stop caring since the course of human activity was set in place billions of years ago. If behavior is fixed in time and space, people will commit horrible sins and crimes without the need to feel any guilt or remorse. In essence, anti-determinists predict bad behavior based on the knowledge that the determined mind's state gladly commits immoral behavior.

This line of thought demonstrates a severe case of doublethink plain and simple because empiricism shows precisely the opposite; that is, human thoughts predict human behavior. Actions inside the mind determine to a large extent movements of the body, telling the person actions have consequences. Guilt results from harming close friends and family, and jails are filled with drug dealers and child molesters. Individuals with multiple sexual partners frequently spread sexually transmitted diseases. In other words, our thoughts and actions often accurately predict our future. Concern that the antideterminist holds about wallowing in the hopeless futility of immoral deterministic view precisely shows how our actions do determine the world.

Thus, despite the repugnance many hold for determinism, there is no fundamental philosophical reason for the atheist to deny determinism at this time, only fear. So consider a determinist's life, hypothetically happy with scientific reasoning as well as being godless, and furthermore caring little about the limits of knowledge. One must logically conclude that this pattern of thought provides no indications of doublethink in itself. In other words, the determinist's mind just does what it does, and all is well with the world. (Evidence remains, however, for other types of doublethinking, to be explained later, and these instances will demonstrate the impossibility of escaping doublethink even for this special person.)

So what do we know? When trying to decide whether or not to jump off the Grand Canyon, empiricism might sound very sensible, while at other times it gets tricky. If alternatives appear unacceptable, then you should explain why empiricism is the case sometimes, and other times it is ignored; because only doublethinkers like me use empiricism when convenient and disregard it later. I say believe in God and determinism both. Use one when plausible and another when not. Never let uniformity cloud the issues nor have a consistent philosophy apply to anyone.

# 5 Skepticism: Life Without a Philosophy

*Socrates is an evildoer, and a curious person, who
searches into things under the earth and in heaven, and
he makes the worse appear the better cause, and he
teaches the aforesaid doctrines to others.*
—SOCRATES'S ACCUSERS

*I neither know, nor think I know.*
—PART OF SOCRATES'S RESPONSE

Inside the mind, old sections of a town still exist, block
after block of run-down factories, dusty warehouses, collaps-
ing stores, and rusting gas stations. Doublethink first condemns
these obsolete structures the way a large city would, calling
them outdated useless heaps. Then doublethink rips out for
recycling the valuable copper and handcrafted woodwork,
using the ornate door hardware, along with the plumbing
fixtures, for the rehabilitation of other sections of the city
not being torn down.

Next comes the wrecking ball. Smashing the dilapidated
buildings to rubble, doublethink salvages old bricks for reuse.
Excavators load trucks with rock and debris bound for the
foundation of the newest development across town; meanwhile removing crusty old structures provides parcels of land

for other uses. Try as it might, doublethink never reduces the mind's town to nothingness.

Throughout history, philosophy and religion helped establish values in each culture. Every society had a guide to right and wrong. Inevitably a person or faction discovers a fault in the system. These people are then called the equivalent of doublethinkers: cynics, sophists, skeptics, infidels, heretics, Christians, anarchists, radicals, Protestants, nihilists, and absurdists.

Usually followers of the existing moral structure falsely accuses the new undesirables of destroying everything by leaving nothing behind, when, in fact, they most definitely sought to replace an old value system with a new one.

Doublethink, the philosophy, doesn't oppose the raw materials needed to assemble the mind, but rather the plan and rules of construction. Doublethink recognizes the crushing of a value system as simply another way to live our lives. With the possible exception of doublethink-induced suicide, doublethink never creates total emptiness, nor could it.

## Skeptics

Doublethink derives in part from prior philosophies, exhibiting common characteristics. Existentialism illustrates an example where followers accept a way of life, not because of provability or necessarily because of it being better, but just for a desire or just for choosing. Nothing ultimately dictates a certain belief, such as the existence of God; therefore, one accepts various rules and lives life. (Existentialists state it differently and often provide long explanations about how it works).

Nihilism, a branch of existentialism, demonstrates similarities as well by saying things like nothing matters, life lacks meaning, no right, no wrong, and so on. Jean Paul Sartre was a nihilist who created much philosophy from being and nothingness (or so I have been told, as he really is quite difficult to follow). Certainly nihilists are interesting and deserving more recognition than I am capable of providing, but others already do them greater justice anyway.

Skepticism, of varying degrees and forms, links doublethink, existentialism, and nihilism. An extreme philosophical skeptic denies everything, while a less extreme individual might question the possibility of certain universal beliefs. Another might suggest that no significant rationalizations can be made, or at least no important or useful ones. A theological skeptic might challenge all forms of religion. Usually we skeptics will distinguish ourselves by criticizing other people's philosophies, proving their beliefs meaningless, inconsistent, or incomplete. We may ridicule Catholics for believing in divine mysteries and having unfounded rituals, or attack a hedonistic philosophy by showing the rules are not followed by the person who claims to hold them. Skeptics find various ideologies 'wrong' in any number of ways. And when skepticism is taken to the extreme position, it approximates a person who accepts doublethink. To a doublethinker like myself, any 'wrong' philosophy indicates nonsense. To go to the next level, if everyone were found 'wrong,' there wouldn't be any legitimate philosophy at all; we would all be full of poppycock. Knowing everyone is 'wrong' is the precise foundation of the doublethink philosophy.

The term 'wrong' certainly needs clarification. A philosophy, for the purpose of demonstrating skepticism (or for this chapter), is knowing with certainty what a person ought to do. It is a group of moral or value judgments, and/or it is a system for making those judgments. Decisions can be made with either a doublethink philosophy or a non-doublethink philosophy. Any philosophy found 'wrong' equates to doublethink, but in order for one to be 'right,' it must meet the following criteria:

1. A philosophy must be provable, or it must be the only set of values a person can have. If a person debates more

than one conflicting belief, then he must 'prove' only one right. If he fails 'proving' a single path correct, he or she does not know which to choose. If uncertain, multiple solutions to the same questions or situations arise, and by default he or she doublethinks. And furthermore if a particular philosophy becomes the only one a person is capable of having, then it must still meet criteria two along with three to demonstrate a 'right' philosophy.

    1a. To 'prove' a philosophy, only consistent, nonconflicting arguments are made since inconsistent, conflicting arguments define doublethink.

2. The philosophy must exhibit internal consistency; in other words, a philosophy must not give more than one answer to the same set of questions. If providing multiple answers, it doublethinks to whatever extent the solutions vary.

3. The application of the philosophy must demonstrate practicality. If a philosophy cannot be applied, then a person responds randomly—correctly or incorrectly, in judgments and/or actions. A person with an unexecuted philosophy doublethinks automatically.

These three rules determine whether a person's outlook on life equates to doublethinks or not. These simple, reasonable conditions prove extremely difficult for belief systems to meet.

Some might anticipate where I am headed and complain this sort of reasoning negates, saying it only seeks to tear apart other people's beliefs: "It builds nothing of its own, offering no hope. If ultimately successful, and carried to its extreme, then no rules endure, allowing skepticism's tomfoolery to criticize folly. Legitimate thinkers ought to question the motives of a person who promotes doublethink. The misleading doublethinker rejoices in confused blabber, unabashedly trying to undermine other philosophies with confusion."

But a doublethink philosopher responds that if demonstrated ultimately true, then so what. "Only doublethink legitimately criticizes the truth of a value system based on subjective preferences. If an individual's reasoning were to be found false, incorrect, or uncertain, it wouldn't reason in the traditional meaning at all; it would simply doublethink."

How does free will stand before the requirements of a 'right' philosophy? Finding its way into many great thinkers' outlooks, free will means that a person makes choices, and these choices are unbounded by physical laws, psychology, economics, and so forth, as well as God or gods. Additionally, these choices are not random.

Suppose a woman confronts a choice between good and evil. Imagine her undaunted by the prospect of going to hell, and she somehow freed herself of all physical as well as non-physical thoughts that may affect her decision. She just freely picks good or evil; her path leads to either hell or heaven, but she gets to select and doesn't care either way. This epitomizes doublethink: two choices but no way to make the decision. But she picks good, evil, or neither, and commits doublethink since she failed to prove one option as the only 'right' path. (Requirement one stated that a 'right' philosophy must select one course of action over another, but free will means removing all the criteria for making a decision—to ensure freedom. Thus free will is not a philosophy, since by its definition it determines nothing.)

Not everyone willingly accepts this proof, so let us continue with free will. Free-willers argue that they make decisions when the facts are presented to the mind. But then by the same reasoning, it could also be argued that mice choose, and virtually every mouse on earth avoids burning if given the option. In addition, humans have fears that ensure their survival because these fears influence decisions. Men do not wish to burn in hell, and given the same options as a mouse, a man would make the identical decision as a lowly rodent, at least with regards to entering an inferno. Furthermore, you could program a robot to do the same, or even a building with a sprinkler system could be said to choose not to burn. Do we conclude that mice, robots, and buildings posses free will?

Why do proclaimers of the gospel find it necessary to insist on the existence of free will, and then detail the devil's faults? Why scare the hell out of someone? If the possibility to frighten the flock of God's sheep away from temptation exists, then how can free will be held responsible for choosing good? The concept of God's omnipotence certainly inspires us to listen to his rules, follow his Bible. But if God created everything and knows all, then how could there be free will? What is free about that? He supposedly created everything including gravity, psychology, and atoms.

How could God be a just god if everyone isn't given the same chance? If he were fair, what necessitates spreading his word? How cruel is God such that he allows one person to grow up in a proper environment, which worships the Lord, and another to flounder in heathen isolation from grace, simply because nobody told him the deal? What twisted form of equality permits one person to see the light, while another witnesses only darkness? If God were good then why does man have free will? Why not make us do the right thing and send everyone to heaven, with eternal bliss? Why give mankind the chance to go smoke, boil, and rot in hell?

In contrast, some people discount the concept of free will. Described in the last chapter, they call themselves determinists. They believe that the world is the way it is, the laws of physics make what we see, and man exhibits no special manner of affecting the dictates of nature. Man falls subject to Mother nature, much like an inert gas. Furthermore, if every significant aspect of a person's mind could be known, then his behavior would also be predicted in advance. Determinism might also involve some random events that could never be formulated, but all human actions cannot conflict the laws of nature, not even once.

Determinism fails to meet the definition of a philosophy in this chapter, since it is not a set of values nor does it make judgments. At best determinism figures out what a person's thought processes include and the resulting behavior. If perfected, it only predicts or explains what is going to happen, saying nothing about what right or wrong consist of. Furthermore, the lack of information and data processing capabilities in the human mind limit determinism's usefulness. The extent to which human behavior can be predicted establishes the boundary of deterministic relevance.

How do determined people act? If we live in a determined world, people make moral judgments and still believe in right and wrong. These decision-making processes are potentially knowable ahead of time, as is everything else. Although not necessarily warranted or good, these fixed value systems are the only philosophy anyone is capable of having. The moral beliefs in such a world likely show inconsistencies (as described later) and thereby demonstrating another form of doublethink. But in the determined point of view, if a person's philosophy demonstrates consistency, then that person could theoretically free him- or herself of doublethink. (Well…in a determined world there is no right or wrong, thus there is no 'right' philosophy.)

This discussion has considered only two basic philosophical positions: free will and determinism. Now take any other philosophical debate—say capitalism versus socialism, pro life versus pro choice, the freedom to practice homosexuality or not—and consider the issue in terms of a 'right' philosophy. I cannot find a single position that stands up without ultimately relying on doublethink. All propositions either make no choices, or they are illogically founded on a preference or desire. Most are also limited by the power of our mind, thus difficult to implement. Furthermore the comprehensive philosophies such as Christianity are riddled with obvious inconsistencies.

## Consistency Over Time

At the risk of redundancy, let's consider another aspect of philosophy with respect to being 'right.' Observations clearly tell us something about an individual's belief system, at least to a limited extent. Values, we can't help but noticing, begin taking shape in the first few years of life. Pain and pleasure are apparent even at birth, followed soon thereafter by all sorts of other new and complex feelings and emotions. In a short time a child possesses a definite set of rules for guiding behavior. Kids know what things they desire, what actions they consider bad, what morals they accept, what they wish to avoid, and what foods they wish to eat. Perhaps later they learn to hate their siblings or drunken neighbors. They often have fear of strangers and avoid darkness. They play with and love puppies and kittens; they enjoy their grandparents' company. When children attend school, they learn to fear the teacher's punishments, while trying to receive praise as well. They experience incompetence, and at other times, they learn to feel that they are somehow different, less able, and unworthy of approval. They normally find friends to play with behind the school or at the roller rink. In fact children learn many, many things, some desirable and some not.

Why is this of such importance to doublethink? Why do Christians usually raise Christians? Why do Muslims raise Muslims? Why do racists raise racists? Why do problem children lead troubled lives? Why do abused children suffer throughout life? Children develop some philosophical characteristics that persist into adulthood. In particular, they begin making judgments at a young age. At such an early developmental stage, little hope exists for children to think anything but doublethink or nonsense, and this early confusion follows them to some extent for the rest of their lives.

Small children experience almost nothing of the world beyond the contrived environments adults allow. They usually cannot read well and have little knowledge of alternative philosophies, instead creating very superficial ideas about God, forever, and justice. The only formal philosophy discovered is what their parents give them or permit to enter their minds. What they almost never do is compare the merits of Christianity with Marxism. They cannot comprehend determinism or atheism in most environments, and would miss Socrates' subtleties even if we tried to enlighten them.

Children may know who Jesus was, but they are not taught that many sincere people think that the "Savior" was not the son of God, and that the decisions of their parents to teach Christianity is in conflict with most of the world. And even if kids were informed of such discrepancies, whom would they choose to follow at such a young age? The parents who nurture and love them, or the strangers who oppose those who protect and feed them? How can a child make the correct decision? Early in life, one is not capable of knowing many important things. What modern four-year-old appreciates the horror of World War II? What six-year-old debates the rules governing courtship or marriage? How many fifteen-year-olds fully comprehend the results of inappropriate sexual behavior, or make the correct decisions? A fifteen-year-old almost universally misinterprets how acts of love and sex evolve to cause joy or suffering for the decades that follow.

But as children enter adulthood, saddled with the decisions of their innocent sheltered beginning and turbulent young adulthood, what opportunities present themselves for a clean break? The decisions of early and late youth will influence middle age and so on. This is not intended to explain how determinism works, but rather it is calling into question all of life. When is a person able to make good decisions about right and wrong? As a preteen, or as an adult, with the residue of being a confused adolescent? No portion of living allows or prepares an individual to make all these decisions free of doublethink. No escape door opens to exit doublethink. Philosophies change throughout life, grow, bend, adapt, accept, open up, and close in. This is healthy, even normal, and yet this is very odd. If a philosophy contains no doublethink, then how can it change? Certainly many examples illustrate consistent changes or non-doublethinking philosophical adjustments. A young lady demonstrates just such a case. During puberty the female body/mind acquires new feelings, emotions, and desires. The flowering woman may gain a desire for sex. Hormonal changes influence philosophy, puberty causes value juggling, and she can still maintain consistency with a new adult outlook on life. Her previous beliefs required no need of detailed rules for petting or reaching the goal of orgasm. Becoming a fully developed person changes the situation/philosophy, and that may be very consistent.

Another non-doublethink change in philosophy sometimes happens during old age. A healthy young man might consider suicide repugnant, but when ninety and in poor health, death provides relief of great physical pain or grief. This type of philosophical change can also show consistency without implying doublethink by itself.

But there are many similar cases when shifts in philosophy indicate definite doublethink. If a girl found sex evil in all cases, but after reaching puberty, having sex, and enjoying it, she changed her mind an incongruity occurred. Sex was either evil in all cases, or it was not. The same could be said of the old man wanting to commit suicide. If the depressed elder abandons a religious faith that says wrapping a rope around our head is wrong, and then hangs himself in the backyard, he doublethinks. Either religious faith correctly guides life in a particular way, or not. Religion seldom subjects itself to newly discovered desires.

## Following a Belief

If we have correct philosophies, then why do we break them so often? Why do some worshipers who attend mass on Sunday, then screw the office assistant on Monday? Do Jews really believe what their sacred scrolls say? Perhaps Communism failed because so few people actually practiced its principles and sacrificed for the common good. Why do empiricists who won't admit superstition avoid thirteens and broken mirrors?

It seems most of us have philosophies in an ideal sense but live in a world full of contradictions to our morals. How many Christians turn the other cheek as Jesus instructed in the Sermon on the Mount? How often do people lie, despite the Ten Commandments (or in some other cases their humanistic values)? Is it a part of their philosophy to lie? Why do so many people believe in heaven, but act like the devil owns their soul? Why do Americans support their government most of the time but are still tempted to cheat on their taxes? How many of us have a belief system only for the sake of having a one, but seldom follow the hard rules?

Using a broken philosophy for the sake of possessing guidelines to live by is very peculiar indeed. Perhaps it was the best you could do? Following a philosophy usually implies a certain amount of consistency and intellectual integrity. Using a set of rules and then ignoring them from time to time seems silly. Why pretend conformity and practice hypocrisy, believing one thing and doing another? Are we really just trying to follow two values that do not fit together? In any case, whenever morality wanders about with your life, then you should just accept the fact that you are doublethinking.

When confronted with a complex dilemma, what do philosophies tell the mind to do? What course of action is appropriate when the rules can't decide? When a code of behavior fails, it indicates one of two problems: First, the system is too difficult to use in a particular case, and if this happens then why bother trying at all? Second, a code could be inconsistent. If various conflicting goals comprise a plan of action, then maybe the objectives don't make sense when carefully considered as a whole. If you have only one significant ending plan, like getting into heaven, then maybe the attack went awry. Regardless, if weaknesses prevent proper moral dilemma resolution, doublethink triumphs again.

If you ever doubt your philosophy then maybe it got sidetracked. If you think your code of ethics seems 'right,' but you never examine it, then perhaps silliness crept in. What legitimate value system allows people to wait for an emotional crisis before questioning their beliefs? Why do Christians try to reconcile with God on their deathbeds? If God's rules are so important then why take that chance? What makes death so difficult to deal with? If your religion correctly defines your goals, wouldn't passing away be a fairly minor event, or even a blessing? Why not accept embalming as a part of being, a transition, or maybe a beginning? Why grieve and wax philosophical near the end of life and feel good a few weeks earlier when you did not know?

Because your philosophy is 'wrong,' inconsistent—bullshit. It never got close. No possible explanations account for ideas you accept as true. You are insincere in all your beliefs and full of scrambled egg thinking. Do you really fully accept your own principles, or are you afraid to question them? Do you fight the doublethink philosophy because you disagree with it or because you loathe it?

Any reasonable approach proves your ethics are false, false, and false. Your actions follow from incorrect thinking. What you use for making decisions does not make sense; rather, it embraces absurdity. You can try to convince yourself that you found a higher plane, but you have not. Because your beliefs are like mashed potatoes and alphabet soup, so are right and wrong. Your value judgments consist of absurdities based on absurdities, never making sense. Every sort of judgment that you have ever made could be 'right,' or it could be 'wrong,' and there is no way of ever knowing. You are confused and morally bankrupt, and if you don't think so, then try to justify your choices fundamentally while following the rules of common sense and simple logic.

# 6 Psychology:
## The Final Argument
## for Doublethink

*Inside outside, Leave me alone.*
*Inside outside, Nowhere is home.*
*Inside outside, Where have I been?*
*Out of my brain on the five fifteen*

—THE WHO, "5:15"

It seems pointless to consider what man ought to do and then ignore what actually gets done. Great thinkers spend lifetimes trying to develop systems to lead us out of the darkness. Frequently, these complex undertakings only confuse and show little relation to how people live and act. The following excerpt comes from Jean-Paul Sartre's *Being and Nothingness*, and represents a typical passage selected from the world-famous philosopher.

> Thus by its very projection toward an end, freedom constitutes as a being in the midst of the world a particular datum which it has to be. Freedom does not choose it, for this would be to choose its own existence; but by the choice which it makes of its end, freedom causes the datum to be revealed in this or that way, in this or that light in connection with the revelation of the world itself. Thus the very contingency of freedom and the world which surrounds this contingency with

its own contingency will appear to freedom only in the light of the end which it has chosen; that is, not as brute existence but in the unity of the illumination on a single nihilation. And freedom would never be able to reapprehend this ensemble as a pure datum, for in that case it would be necessary that this freedom be outside of all choice and therefore that it should cease to be freedom (Sartre [1956] 1966, 626).

The reason for quoting Sartre is not to poke fun at a dead man, but rather for illustrating the difficulty of understanding some belief systems. Apparently his followers thought he had something important to say. Sadly, most of us will never know what it was. Even if Sartre wrote about things that could make a difference, what good did he do by using a writing style that confuses almost everyone who reads it? Among other problems is that he uses convoluted language, extrapolating new definitions for ordinary words. He might just as well have written a book about doublethink. Or maybe he did.

Despite Sartre's inability to clarify the meaning of life for most of us, his advocacy for free will seems apparent in the bulk of his work. He obviously thought free will essential since he mentions the concept numerous times. But, for the sake of argument, consider the possibility that Sartre chose the wrong side; imagine the activities of the human mind prove predictable. Can empirical study, utilizing psychological insights, reveal characteristics of a person's value system? Does psychology explain the flaws of a particular belief or even philosophy in general?

Studying what people do and have done, emphasizing actual behavior, psychology could provide a tool to measure philosophy. Consider the following propositions:

- A philosophy that is psychologically impossible to follow is doublethink.

- Inconsistent psychological behavior can indicate an inconsistent philosophy (or doublethink).

At this point, a psychological model will provide a beginning for answering the questions from previous chapters. The model that follows, while not all-encompassing, explains how the mind functions in limited situations. This simple look at life bases it reasoning on common experiences. The descriptions are intended to lend insight into the psychology of doublethink, and the nonsense found in philosophy in general.

## The Model of the Mind

*1. Feelings and emotions guide thoughts (to a limited extent).*

Essentially the mind registers stimulation in some way. The stimulation causes the mind to bring up a number of "emotional reports" for consideration. All of the alternatives or solutions, under consideration, are weighed according to the values in their "emotional reports."

A woman named Vicky goes to bed. The coldness of the bedroom stimulates her skin causing an assessment of the situation, and to compare the options at hand. She thinks about the pain suffered on other chilly nights prompting a negative reaction. Then she thinks about how blankets have kept her warm in the past, creating a positive feeling, and so Vicky covers herself with a thick quilt. The emotions associated with comforting thoughts outweighed those associated with coldness and goose bumps. Many ideas in the mind come with a set of emotions attached. Coldness recalls a memory of previous pain suffered due to a broken furnace, also connecting to a remembrance of the warmth created with a blanket. These emotions and feelings helped her mind to make a decision.

Often the process weaves its way through several layers of thoughts attached to other emotions. The following afternoon Vicky waits to turn at a stoplight, pausing because of not wanting to get a ticket. She associates traffic violations with inconvenience and embarrassment, but she is also anxious to get to school to see her daughter. Vicky feels happy knowing her child learns at Kennedy Elementary, but really wants to hold her daughter and relive pleasant memories of her darling little angel. All these emotions operate inside Vicky's mind. She evaluates several of them simultaneously, or nearly so. Once the light changes color, she moves on both physically and mentally to the next obstacle on her journey.

*2. The mind selectively exaggerates or amplifies emotional reports and stimuli in general.*

The mind receives stimuli then decides which ones cause anxiety, fear, anger, joy, happiness, and so on, also choosing which to diminish, ignore, or set on hold. In other words, the mind manipulates the intensity of the emotions attached to the various inputs.

A great deal of practical evidence supports this phenomenon actually happening. Consider the small child who falls down the stairs but does not start crying until she realizes her grandmother witnessed the accident. If the pain alone sufficed to cause the strong emotions of crying, then the child would have shed tears regardless of whether or not her grandmother watched. The child's mind received the stimuli of pain, decided it unworthy of crying over, and then realized Grandmother's presence along with her empathetic hug eases the suffering. Finally, in an attempt to guarantee Grandma's attention, the child chose to exaggerate the emotions that lead to crying.

Other types of variation in mood demonstrate amplification in stimulation. When a well-rested parent plays with a two-year-old child, great joy results. The small person's behavior seems cute, funny, and pleasant. In contrast after a long day's work, a parent changes and reacts with anger at the dinner table antics of his or her offspring. In this type of instance, unrelated activities stressed the mind. Tension dictated that the parent no longer accept certain types of behavior. In these extreme cases, the responsible adult becomes enraged by one sort of two-year-old conduct, which at another time caused laughter and merriment. The mind amplifies emotions as well as feelings—and exaggerates selectively. Stress for the mom or dad provided the motivation for the attitude shift toward frustration.

*3. The mind stimulates itself—or at least after the excitations have stopped coming in it still functions and experiences emotions.*

Dreams provide an obvious example. The mind experiences strange hallucinations all through the night, with virtually no outside stimulation present to provide input. While lying in bed having a nightmare about falling from a tall building, George could actually rest in the basement of a one-story house. Perhaps during a walk past the Sears Tower building earlier in the day, the thought of falling from the top gave him pause to consider such an event. Or possibly George carries a latent fear of heights set into place by a chain of events twenty-two years ago: He climbed a stepladder as a child and slipped over the top, landing on his face. The key here is the mind's power to conjure up emotions, ideas, and visions, when the objects that originally may have created the idea no longer physically present themselves. The mind in essence thinks about something not currently happening.

Another example is remembering. While sitting at home, George contemplates a situation at work. The assistant manager recalls the anxious crowd that appeared at the Brown Olive Restaurant following the football game. George asked waiters and waitresses to come in to work without advance notice to take care of the upset customers packing the lobby. Later while lying on the couch and reflecting on the long line of customers standing in the lobby of the restaurant, he experiences the same fear and upset stomach from six hours earlier.

For the purpose of this model it does not matter if the emotions pertaining to work ultimately connect to identifiable external stimuli, but that the mind self-creates fantasies and feelings. In other words, it energizes itself on visions and events for which no excitations currently enter the body.

4. *The mind blocks some stimuli (perhaps not actually blocking the stimuli directly, but instead diminishing the feelings and emotions associated with certain stimuli to the point that they loose significance).*

Take the case of George's next very busy day. He forgot about lunch during the rush. Normally the stomach gives the hunger signal about eleven o'clock. For the next fifteen minutes George's brain amplifies the stimuli and feels a strong appetite. Usually George endures the hunger pains until about eleven-fifty, stops managing his employees, walks to the kitchen, fixes a ham sandwich, and pours a glass of milk. But on the day when two waitresses came to work late, he never ate lunch. George's frustration overcame the normal routine because the customers were upset, and the cook in the kitchen kept mixing up the orders, even sprinkling garlic in the ice cream. Somehow George's mind forgot completely about eating this day. Thus his mind intercepted the hunger stimuli and concentrated on more urgent matters. Later that evening George does not even recall feeling lunchtime hunger.

5. *The mind also has the ability of blocking its own stimuli.*

This important skill is demonstrated when a person thinks about a problem with a number of possible solutions. The mind decides for whatever reason to delve only into a couple of the numerous conceivable answers. With all the other plausible options still present, it simply turns off the stimulation for the ones it does not like. The mind won't force itself to ponder details of each idea; it merely excludes the 'bad' ones from further consideration. If the other "good" ideas fail it can simply turn the memories from the "bad" ideas back on again.

After George's series of unpleasant experiences he decides to take a trip to a ski resort. George talks to several airlines United, American, Northwest, and so on. Finally George decides to purchase the cheapest tickets with only one connecting flight in St. Louis. After George selects American he quickly forgets about Northwest, United, and the others. He now only tries to remember that his flight departs Thursday at 8 A.M., as well as where the tickets are stored, next to bed in a drawer. Meanwhile George makes plans for a hotel room to stay in, and then visits the sporting goods store to purchase bindings and new poles. George no longer mentally hashes out airline schedules but instead finalizes preparations for this trip.

Unfortunately, the evening before the adventure was to begin, the Weather Channel forecasts a massive snowstorm in St. Louis. Luckily George purchased refundable tickets. He can now call the other airlines and make arrangements for an alternate route, thereby avoiding the entire mess. George suddenly remembers United Airline's flight with a plane change in Chicago. He even recalls the schedule approximately coincides with American; so George phones United and books the flight.

In terms of the model, George considered the problem of arranging for a plane ticket and then narrowed his focus down to one airline. When the chosen airline developed problems the night before departure, it caused a recollection of previously excluded stimuli regarding alternative travel schedules. Or more simply, George blocked stimuli from "bad" ideas, then unblocked the stimuli of these very same ideas.

*6. The mind uses the ability to selectively block or receive as well as amplify or diminish, its own thoughts, to focus in on prioritized stimuli or emotions.*

When a person focuses or concentrates, he or she actually exaggerates a group of stimuli associated with a particular idea, and likewise diminish others. The mind sensitizes itself to react more strongly toward what it perceives to be important thoughts. This concept can be represented in Michael's behavior. As the young man watches a football game on TV, his thoughts primarily follow the game. The timer on the oven suddenly rings a third time. The stimulation of the ringing causes a shift in focus. The new concentration covers the mental hub surrounding the pizza—which Michael had recently forgotten—and then a plan to pull it out of the oven, and finally a strategy to put the pizza in a safe place. All ideas and emotions surrounding saving the pizza receive exaggeration. Much of the other normal stimulation of the football game gets blocked, since it does not pertain to the immediate crisis of burning food. A few minutes later, with the pizza emergency resolved, Michael returns to the couch and resumes viewing the game. Thus the mind selectively ignored the game to focus on pizza crisis, then reversed itself.

*7. The mind smooths over certain unpleasant thoughts by shifting focus.*

Picture Mary after a troubling day of work, resting on the couch, her mind relaxing and ignoring the troubles of the day. Although those fading memories were extremely important earlier in the morning, Mary's mind now eases and de-emphasizes them, soothing the headache by focusing on the peaceful and pleasant thoughts of her domestic lifestyle. Not that this is a universal experience, but it often happens when a person no longer confronts an immediate crisis, the focus shifts into other areas. In many cases, the escape essentially means ignoring or avoiding the difficult situations of the day by using the removal of the external stimuli. It also includes a reorientation toward thinking about calm, serene images.

8. *The mind shifts focus from one area to the next and at the same time taking care of certain actions with a function resembling autopilot.*

The brain executes many routine tasks with mental focus elsewhere. While walking down the street, a woman thinks about what she intends to buy at the supermarket. Next she tries to remember what time she told her husband she would return from the store. While crossing the street she sees a billboard on the side of a bus advertising the show she wants to see. Throughout the entire trip, her basic path to the store was never interrupted. She used autopilot to get to the store and never gave it any thought.

## Put It all Together

With the model laid out in items one through eight, it is possible to draw a relationship between doublethink and how the mind functions. Of particular importance are items six through eight's methods of shifting focus—a truly wonderful phenomenon. I could never have written this book if I did not focus on doublethink. It was helpful to diminish thoughts of unrelated areas while considering the merits of Sartre versus Freud. No mere human dwells on his sister's recent divorce, anguishes over the health of an ailing grandmother, occupies himself with thoughts of a day job, and meanwhile writes a decent book on philosophy. In addition, I must frequently put aside thoughts of my wife and children during the creative process.

But these "distractions" of family and job are all usually valued highly by me, so I am forced to shift priorities. That presents no problem, because the mind can do this. I enjoyed writing this book, so I made a time to concentrate fully on writing. I allowed myself this relief from putting kids to bed and loading the dishwasher.

Sometimes I have acted with less than pure motives. Visiting taverns I shuffled my scruples around in other ways. I flirted with various women; at the same time forgetting the pain my friend's messy breakup caused him. I enjoyed intoxication, and selectively ignored the fact that work performance the next day dropped with each beer I drank. My grandmother's health seemed distant and unimportant. I also let go of the thoughts about the pain inflicted on my family by staying out so late. These shifts were not random, since I was intentionally trying to break my own laws, enjoying certain types of rotten tavern behavior and trying to find a path to them.

To further illustrate, consider Peter. Peter's mind knows that it wants sex, and it knows how to find it. At most times it ignores lewd impulses by making rules against certain types of sexual behavior. Perhaps Peter wishes to avoid breaking the vows of marriage, so during Sunday's services he decides on a principle to follow: "I will not have sex with anyone other than my wife." This feels good when first expressed, but he might not follow it. Later in the week Peter realizes he wants to grope a receptive woman he just met, and now needs to reorganize his morals; he can do that! In fact Peter cannot avoid this sort of behavior in some cases, namely every time he places himself in a certain environment (a singles bar). With the aid of alcohol he changes into a sex-craved, adolescent-like fool, exaggerating the emotions connected with infidelity.

In Peter's case (and everyone else's for that matter) the mind can simply tell right and wrong to take a leap. Values can change with a moment's notice. People generally assume that behavior remains somewhat logical and stable. But real world experience shows we do not stack principles in a permanent fashion.

Philosophers, however, in their contrived worlds, tend to place principles in sorts of lists; if not actual lists, then they at least they imply hierarchy. They use phrases like "the highest good" or "the purest thoughts," with the follower then understanding which actions or thoughts to put first. The list below illustrates what a philosopher might suggest to follow. Example A:

1. I am a hedonist first and foremost.
2. I can best promote my hedonism by being a humanist.
3. I demand that others do not contradict humanism, at least not to any significant degree, which, in fact, reinforces my own humanism.
4. I enjoy family, and it ordinarily poses no great threat to my hedonism or my humanistic values, therefore I shall have a family.
5. A monogamous lifestyle satisfies my hedonistic sex drive while seldom disrupting my generally humanistic and family frame of living.
6. Working contradicts hedonism, but it also allows for the accumulation of wealth, which can be dispensed for either humanistic goals, for my family, or for many types of hedonism.
7. I enjoy drinking, but I shall not let it overtake my humanistic impulses. In addition, excessive drinking decreases the amount of hedonistic pleasure enjoyed.
8. And so on and so forth down to the finer points.

This outline shows a strictly hypothetical plan that is strictly nonsensical crap. Values are dynamic. All of the items on the list will at various times be ignored, placed at the top, bottom, and somewhere in the middle of the list. In an abstract manner of rationalizing behavior, it may seem convenient to organize a philosophy in this manner, but this process misleads, since no human allows his or her outlook to stay in any fixed order.

At certain times the individual with such a plan is compelled to ignore the love of his family for the sake of his work. At other times his wife and children bring great hardship, sorrow, and pain, which in turn contradicts his hedonism.

Sometimes while intoxicated he forgets to consider his young children. Sometimes he purchases products that are connected to non-humanitarian causes, knowingly buying a Christmas present manufactured with the slave labor of imprisoned Chinese human rights activists and selecting tobacco products from a company that promotes an unhealthy habit to children.

In light of the psychological model, a more accurate philosophical structure would place values in clumps. A value clump represents a set of thoughts that are bound together by events and emotions. The organization of these thoughts resembles clumps of dirt. Both are uneven, of different sizes, of differing consistency, are constantly breaking apart and reattaching, and in addition they are generally only crudely predictable in their interactions with other value clumps. A person could have the following menus of clumps for various occasions:

| **Church** | **Football** |
|---|---|
| Love of God | Winning |
| Avoid sin | Toughness |
| Peace | Desire |
| Security | Passion |
| Family | Excitement |
| Love | Loyalty |
| Joy | Teamwork |
| Discipline | |
| Anxiety toward shortcomings | |

| **Tavern** | **An intruder in the house** |
|---|---|
| Sex | Panic |
| Alcohol | Anxiety |
| Excitement | Anger |
| Freedom | Fear |
| Hangover/pain | |

In terms of the above groups, the following scenario depicts a likely series of events: During a church service a worshiper experiences one set of emotions/values. His love of God inspires concrete guidelines to live by. Each and every Sunday, his fellow parishioners help create an environment where serious, thoughtful soul searching discourages sin. Later in the afternoons during football games the same worshiper turns into a Packers' fan and encounters a very different set of emotions. Now he becomes angry at officials, impatient with the quarterback, and secretly happy when the opposing team's wide receiver reinjures an ankle.

Unquestionably any given person would not need to have any of these particular clumps, but still he or she follows some patterns of shifting principles and beliefs. In fact, every functioning, conscious person uses various types of value clumps. The mind's shifting focus necessitates changing values. In terms of the model, values consist of groups of stimuli or emotions that intensify or diminish, depending on the situation. The mind amplifies desires as needed, allowing a hungry person to wish for food highly enough to stop other activities and wait at a restaurant table, a thirsty child to increase her desire for water, and a man's wish for sex to increase in the presence of an attractive woman, as well. Thus, a system of organized and constant values, regardless of the structure, would prove psychologically impossible, since any set of values places itself at the mercy of moving about. At best a person obeys a fluid set of beliefs roughly controlled by the human mind and the external world.

Imagine the implementation of another set of structured morals. Consider Richard, a devout Christian and the father of two boys. Richard strived to treat his children in a firm, consistent, and loving manner. When his two sons failed to measure up to his high standards, he delivered punishments and taught lessons intended to correct the behavior in an expedient manner. When the elder son was arrested for possession of marijuana, Richard took control of the situation.

He prayed and then educated himself on this type of drug use, severely admonished his son, and found better methods of monitoring the older child's behavior. The experience scared Richard for he feared he might lose his first son to a drug addiction.

Three years later the second son had a similar incident; the younger child began hanging around known drug users. At this point in time Richard lost control of his emotions and went to a different clump. First he verbally abused the child, then angrily beat him. The ability to attack his own son is not a behavior for which Richard normally wished. Richard's ferocious behavior, paired with anger, sharply contrasts his previously used thoughtful, firm and consistent method of discipline. Richard in both cases wanted to keep his boys free of drug use, but this time Richard's program of self-control went out the window. Richard lost compassion he desired for most of the time out of frustration inspired by a fear of drug usage by his two sons. Richard discovered a new optional behavioral pattern, a new clump.

With Richard, or rather people in general, some clumps blend consistently with each other while some clash. Family meshes with Church, fitting together well, as would Tavern to Drunkenness. Family and Frustration, however, do not make a good match. When Christians are frustrated, they sometimes ignore the gospels altogether, often using devilish thoughts to guide their behavior.

Conceivably for a Christian, the only life free of conflicting values would be in a cloistered convent or a monastery. Such a place seeks to simplify a person's existence, by limiting contradiction, reducing exposure to opposing outlooks on life. All the ideals in an isolated religious environment more or less direct lifestyles toward wholesome, religious experiences. Is all evil eliminated in this environment? Of course not. In fact, Christianity claims that all people sin, cannot avoid sin, and are compelled to disobey from time to time. Christians should instead admit (and perhaps they sort of do) that values are mixed up and that every human being doublethinks. Nietzsche (not a Christian) wrote: "Even among those whose objective is only their own moral purification, among hermits and monks, there can be found such savage and morbid men, hollowed out and consumed by failure" (Nietzsche [1873–76] 1997, part 4).

It is futile for Christians to try to eliminate all outside evil influences, because everyone practices mixed-up philosophy. In other words conflicting desires find their way into a nun's soul as they do into a prostitute's heart. Christians can only seek to reduce certain types of conflicting actions and avoid certain thoughts.

In contrast, if the devil ran an isolated community for the purpose of promoting evil, he might eliminate exposure to goodness and kindness. But even while committing the most horrendous acts in this evil paradise, I think it would still be possible for his wicked followers to have feelings of tenderness and compassion.

Doublethink accepts all this philosophical nonsense. Of course an admitted doublethinker like myself still could try to organize his philosophy, pretending to act in a certain consistent manner, feeling limited anxiety at not knowing what his topsy-turvy values will cause him to do. In a strange way, a list of rules might give a committed doublethinker comfort. (My priorities could include: Life is confused, silliness good, consistency evil, and so on.) Perhaps this plan will take me through troubled times, leading to something better in life.

It is safe to presume that most people wish for the existence of a singlethink philosophy. I sometimes do. But knowing I wish for consistency should only make me more suspicious that my beliefs are simply confirming what I want to be true. Longing for a consistent philosophy does not make a person capable of having a clump system that complies with this need; but the frank acknowledgment reality of my shrimp gumbo philosophies is disturbing. Not having one list of right and wrong appears to lead to a very difficult life, regardless of human limitations.

It comforts a woman to think she will never commit murder. This motivates her to want to avoid murdering every single day. But if homicide falls into one of her clumps, then it gets difficult to avoid axing a drunken husband, when anger calls that clump to the forefront. This vile act shocks most people, but if the clump exists and it receives the message, it happens.

By contrast not all clumps affect such profound change in one's marital status; in fact, most clumps sound very mundane when described. But studying these sorts of mental actions and understanding how they function verifies that confusion permeates all behaviors. The following list of thoughts shows the structure for a formal philosophy:

- Being fat makes me uncomfortable.
- Large thighs make me unattractive.
- I want to lose my large rear end.
- I must eat less ice cream.
- I must jog three miles today.

Compare to this list of reality clumps:
- I am hungry.
- I must eat pizza and a banana split.
- I really must eat the pepperoni and mozzarella.
- I really, really must eat anything.
- I don't care about my fat jelly belly.
- I am tired.
- I grow more tired with each step.
- I must stop this running.
- I must rest now on the park bench.
- I don't care about my cellulite.

The naive dieter/philosopher lists a set of prioritized values, then faces reality. The poor soul aspires to weight loss but has times when the highest goals are trampled upon. She expects to have a plan, but it breaks down. She follows one particular set of desires while planning weight reduction on a full stomach, and another set of cravings while ordering pizza with hunger pains. This is doublethink.

Many people conceptualize their thought processes in a nice straight orderly list, but in reality they waffle all over the place, with every sort of rule jumbled. Rapists, for example, probably have moments when they feel unwanted approaches are very wrong, and also instances of lust when they find it very pleasant. Unfortunately, this leads to mixed results since simply having an itemization of values most of the time is not sufficient to avoid prison.

Inconsistency causes no problems for the philosophy of doublethink because you can build a philosophical system emphasizing virtue and the highest form of noble purity, and then just ignore it whenever. Or perhaps do not ignore it; simply amend it when needed, append, agonize; drive yourself insane with the failures. And if the Christian God resides at or near the top of the program, then there is a convenient rule that allows for suspending the system from time to time. Simply ask the father in heaven for his forgiveness later.

Values dance about the brain, spinning and turning. Frustration and fear cause even the most saintly prude to sin as all principal twists, collapses, and twists again. Only quicksand and mush fill the skull, allowing no sane place to exist, nor any fixed rules to reside. Only nonsense endures. Psychological limitations prevent structure in philosophy, thus all philosophy reduces to quagmire. A philosophy presupposes unobtainable psychological requirements can be met—thus guaranteeing doublethink retaining control.

# Beginning, Middle, and End

The psychological states of the individual in many ways provide the beginning, middle, and end of philosophy. Psychological constraints determine which philosophical issues are debated. Once establishing the area under consideration, predictable mental processes control the decision-making. Finally, other psychological limits dictate how the rules are implemented. Value clumps at every stage govern philosophy.

In the beginning of a philosophical movement, one often looks for avoidance of some appalling action. When white police officers beat a black crime suspect, the NAACP sponsors demonstrations and protests. Racism provides a natural target for a responding moral clump to form inside a young African American man. It troubles him and many others to see friends and neighbors harassed or tortured. Personal tranquility comes from visions of tolerance, harmony, understanding, and cooperation—thus providing a psychological motive for wishing to end racism and prejudice. Such was the basis of what Dr. Martin Luther King, Jr., taught and guided a particular young man.

During the debate (middle) of ethics, a person necessarily abides in a clump of some sort. After recently watching a television special on the bloody assassination of Dr. King, the moralizing young man salts his general outlook with anger and hostility (despite King's calls for nonviolence). Clearly the image of murder changes his consideration of all aspects of his soft-spoken tolerance. Thus while debating what is right and wrong about the treatment of minorities, he must also confront the bitterness inflicted upon his soul by the evil deeds of murdering bigots.

Finally after a person has proposed the topic for a philosophy to fix, and then debated it, comes the implementation. In this case, a follower of King decided to attend a counter-demonstration against the Ku Klux Klan.

Certainly if anything can put a peace-loving-anti-racist-pacifist in an unfamiliar clump it will be the KKK. After an hour of yelling and chanting in hopes of drowning out the Imperial Wizard, the young King devotee finds a chunk of granite in his hand. He launches the gray rock at the white hoods; a quantum shift in values occurred, flip-flopping away from King's teachings.

To sum it up, a philosophical stand requires a mindset that allows for its creation. Without such a window of opportunity a moral stand never occurs within the individual. While the new position is mentally debated, the clumps that take place during the debate necessarily color it. Once the notion gains acceptance, and some set of events transpire requiring the implementation of a philosophical plan, the outcome submits to the mercy of the state the individual currently resides in. And particularly if the implementation of a belief is highly sensitive to anger, frustration, fear, and so forth, it may, in fact, cause the stand to have an undesirable affect—in some cases precisely the opposite of what the mind intended when accepting the original position.

It was earlier established that it is psychologically impossible to have a consistent hierarchy of values. At this point it has been further demonstrated that any attempt to create philosophy, debate philosophy, and to use philosophy is necessarily tainted by the present accompanying mental state. There is nothing pure about philosophy since it is subject to the whims of emotion. Any philosophy afflicted with convoluted priorities indicates doublethink. Philosophy is doublethink.

On the other hand one could simply ignore this problem, develop a set of rules, debate it or not, then use it or ignore it. Why argue that one type of thinking contains more doublethink than another? Doublethink is doublethink is life. Do not concern yourself with issues like consistency and logic. Clearly no meaningful solution exists without relying on absurdity. Obviously a compromised mind gives the best and only solutions and all the alternatives are less reliable, sensible, or valid. Philosophy is doublethink, so why not believe anything? This is freedom.

# 7 Clumps:
## An Empirical Look at How the Mind Doublethinks

*If Butter cups buzz'd after the bee,*
*If boats were on land, churches on sea,*
*If ponies rode men and if grass ate the cows,*
*And cats should be chased into holes by the mouse,*
*If the mamas sold their babies*
*To the gypsies for half a crown;*
*If summer were spring and the other way round,*
*Then all the world would be upside down.*

—SONGWRITER UNKNOWN,
"THE WORLD TURNED UPSIDE DOWN"

The first six chapters of this book more or less found doublethink to be a philosophy of default. And because no brain escapes the eggbeater, I have proposed just accepting it. But acknowledging a set of beliefs that has more in common with insanity than wisdom will still not satisfy most. Thus the search continues for a better answer to what it is we really know for sure.

Fortunately, you must suspect there are other faces to the philosophy of doublethink, if for no other reason than to account for the behavior of the author. Why hasn't the writer of this book gone mad? What prevented his free fall into incoherent blabbering?

It turns out wanting to dwell in the abyss of doublethink does not create acute psychosis. Hoping to slip permanently into irrational chatter makes little difference in one's ability to do so. Although we can be confident of the psychological impossibility of eliminating everyday mental lapses into gibberish, this chapter argues for the equally difficult proposition of embracing nonsense as an absolute philosophy. Or from another perspective, my own experiences show little chance for a committed doublethinker abandoning all sense of the world. (But if a person could completely embrace the concept of overt misthinking, then the rest of this book just rambles on mindlessly, unnecessarily, and devoid of meaning. [There is no reason to assume that such a person would still be reading anyway.])

The previous chapter introduced value clumps, helping to explain the complexity of consistently applying a fixed set of morals. While the existence of value clumps creates problems for philosophers, they also provide structure, as complicated it may be. To find something useful in this mixed-up mess it is first essential to understand what mental clumps are. (Value clumps are really just a specific type [subset] of mental clumps.) The rest of this chapter defines the properties of mental clumps.

In terms of the mind, a clump is:

1. The mental state a person is in.
2. A group of rules constraining one's behavior while in that mental state.
3. Focusing on a group of thoughts, stimuli, memories, and so forth.
4. Temporary and evolving.
5. Usually partially dependent on stimuli outside the mind. Examples of stimuli that can affect clumps and are external to the mind—hunger; pain of all types; bodily feedback

from mental activity, nervousness, excitement, and so forth; vision; sound; taste; smell; and touch.

6. Always dependent on internal mental excitation. Examples of self-generated activity from inside the mind include visualization and memories of past sounds, sights, smells, feeling, taste, anger, love, joy, hunger, and so forth. (Amplification of stimuli can be a combination of internal amplification of an initial external source excitation.)

7. Connected to other clumps.

8. Either very specific and narrow, or a group of behaviors somehow linked together. (The term covers both cases.)

9. Capable of the full spectrum of emotional intensity.

10. Self-restricting in movement toward other unpleasant clumps, while self-encouraging in movement toward other enjoyable ones.

11. A memory in some cases. In general, memories consist of clumps that when active, cause a limited mental recreation of past events.

12. Pleasant in some cases, unpleasant in others.

13. Deceptive at times.

14. Normally only loosely constrained by philosophical rules.

15. Not obligated to be consistent with other clumps.

16. Dynamic.

17. Repetitive at times (sometimes only approximately, but other times nearly exactly the same as previously executed clumps). This kind of behavior is called a habit, or sometimes a bad habit, or even a mental illness.

18. Limited in size. A person only activates a certain number and size of clumps at any one period of time, much like a computer only performs so many tasks at once before running out of processing capacity and RAM.

19. Able to form into groups of protective layers to prevent other specific clumps from occurring.

20. Often destabilized by intentional doublethink, as well as unfamiliar stimuli. Destabilized clumps usually quickly and anxiously return to the more familiar locations—but sometimes move into other clumps that are normally avoided.

21. Less predictable when destabilized.

22. Often less logical with respect to itself when viewed as a large group of clumps that are simultaneously activated; often more logical with respect to itself when viewed as a smaller number of clumps activated.

23. Frequently limited in scope by fatigue and other similar types of constraints. A tired state reduces the locations the mind can visit to increase the possibility of rest. An energetic state allows or encourages the mind to move toward the areas requiring more physical activity and emotions.

24. Often looking for patterns. Unless a strong mental activity, associated with being exact dominates, a person usually accepts approximations as equivalent to identical.

25. Not always active. (When inactive clumps tend to decrease in intensity, detail, and scope.)

26. Often a memory, which is usually more vivid if the source event originally occurred when strong emotions were present.

27. Old or new. When old, and/or inactive, a memory clump can be pieced back together with other related clumps as well as external stimuli, such as someone reminding you of the known facts surrounding a series of long passed events.

28. Reconstructed sometimes. These clumps can vary significantly from the way the events originally occurred. (Unfortunately this characteristic has the side effect of forcing the mind to rely on inaccurate memories.)

29. Sometimes a memory that gains in detail when the events that created it are repeated. (Living in the same house for several years allows a person to memorize the interior to a significantly greater extent than a person who visits only once.)

30. Sometimes a task. When actions are repeated often, the mind takes short cuts, no longer looking for details previously required to obtain a desired object. The thought process bypasses repetitive decisions as it travels through routine superficial patterns. It eliminates whole sequences of intermediate memories and other considerations and jumps to a final action (task). (If the intermediate and ignored considerations are logical in nature and necessary, the process can skip past them as well. Thus, the mind can perform illogical behavior by this means.)

31. Occasionally for delivering anxious feelings as the result of being in close proximity of another emotionally laden clump. Opportunity for anxiety tends to create a more intense, quicker consideration of possible actions. In other words, if a person almost reaches a highly stimulated state (i.e., sex), the mind acts like the accelerator on a car—the car speeds up (but a fast-moving car is not necessarily under control). The mind races to consider different options with the excitement adding extra energy in an attempt to achieve the desired state (i.e., climax). By a similar means it can avoid unpleasant stimulation.

32. Affected by alcohol, causing a person to have thoughts and actions not normally considered. Alcohol alters the entire process, diminishing certain stimuli, including vitally important pain signals, and then at the same time it often amplifies other inputs such as sentimentality. The normal mental functions seem to come back when the drinker sobers up. Visiting intoxication clumps, however, can also cause long-term and profound changes in the

behavior. (I believe other drugs have comparable effects, but I have no direct personal knowledge.)

33. Usually searching for a simplified plan. If a mind finds a way to achieve a desired clump in an easier manner, such as using cocaine or drinking beer, it may choose intoxication frequently and compulsively.

## Common Clumps Examples

Watching a favorite television program: Specifically this process consists of contemplating the actions of the characters on the show, focusing both eyes on the screen, listening attentively to the dialogue, ignoring the other people in the room, sitting comfortably, and avoiding unrelated stimuli in general.

Making love: While in this mode lovers tend to concentrate on a partner's sexual organs, arousing thoughts and memories of previous tantalizing encounters, paying close attention to one's own bodily stimuli, shutting the television off to avoid distractions, and focusing on other related details.

Recalling the events of a crime: This includes a witness mentally retracing the various steps of the incident, visualizing the criminal's face, placing the locations of key items such as the gun and getaway car, sequencing the events in a logical order, and blocking out thoughts of washing laundry and shoe shopping.

A narrow clump: When Jill sees an elevator, she becomes very anxious and nervous.

A broader clump: While standing in a hotel lobby, Jill notices a bank of elevators while a group of old classmates enters the lobby. A nervous and excited Jill anticipates talking to her friends and feels a cool draft passing through the doors. Simultaneously a hotel clerk tries to get her to sign the credit card slip for the room payment.

From a psychological perspective, it sometimes works better (proves more useful) to talk in broader terms and sometimes in narrower terms. It might help to isolate the thoughts about elevators, or to instead talk only about hotel front desk behaviors.

## The Bigger Picture

Some clumps cause disruptive behavior. Suppose Billy, a six-year-old child, sees his toddler sister die from falling out of an apartment window. The thought so horrifies the young boy that over the course of the next few months he builds up several clumps to avoid thinking about the pain of witnessing his sister's death. One clump seeks to avoid leaving windows open around small children. Another encourages visions of her not as a blotch of body parts on the sidewalk below, but rather as an angel in heaven. Billy is ill equipped to deal with this type of trauma, as are most people, so he surrounds the most painful thoughts with a blockade.

The following diagram illustrates a group of clumps associated with his sister's fall:

```
3           3           3           3           3
2 2 2 2 2 2 2 2 2 2 2 2 2 2 2 2 2 2 2 2 2
3 2 1 1 1 1 1 1 1 1 1 1 1 1 1 1 1 1 1 2
3 2 1 H o r r i b l e M e m o r y 1 2 3
3 2 1 1 1 1 1 H 1 1 1 1 1 1 1 1 1 1 1 1 2
2 2 2 2 2 2 2 H 2 2 2 2 2 2 2 2 2 2 2 3
3           3           H           3           3           3
```

Visiting the horrible memory creates the tier-one clumps. In this case Billy, may seek to avoid seeing the window since the glass opening can lead to thoughts of his sister's collision. Because of this potential mental path, Billy attaches pain to the memory clumps of the window. Whenever he thinks about the window, he grows anxious and may start to cry to avoid the next step of remembering his sister's death. Thus, he establishes tier-one clumps to prevent the mind from going on to the horrible memory.

Tier-two clumps prevent travel to tier one. In Billy's case, the multiple tiers could include going into the room with the window, since he previously attached pain to the passageways to the earth below. He, in turn, also associates pain with going near the room.

Tier-three clumps prevent a person from reaching tier-two clumps. Tier-three clumps are simply one more level removed from the initial horrible memory.

H offers a path not currently blocked. If Billy reaches any of the H's he can again experience the horrible memory. Seeing a picture of his sister looking out the window might cause reaching an H.

This system illustrates a compromise, namely that Billy continues to live a calmer existence, but he must also avoid certain clumps passionately to maintain his tranquility. If Billy's friends sense his edginess and tease him into tier two, it could create another horrible experience, and this potential requires another layer of barricades. Should the inconsiderate playmates repeatedly harass him about these newly created painful locations (and the old ones too), he can eventually have his safe sphere of existence effectively reduced to a very small, anxiety laden minefield for set of clumps. In other words, Billy's horrible memory could lay a foundation for more anxious and angry reactions. The antagonizing from others could lead to the number of bad responses to increasing significantly, including hitting or withdrawal.

By itself, the horrible memory at the root of this problem is not necessarily disruptive in the young man's life. The clumps surrounding it, however, either make or break Billy. If he confronts the fears in the neighboring areas and triumphs over them, the actual pain will resurface and be dealt with again. If not, there is no guarantee of anything.

(Ironically when I first devised this scheme, I assumed that nobody would want to dwell in the anxiety clumps, but now I know sometimes we do, since it is exciting, stimulating, even interesting. It appears to take some practice, but a person can exist indefinitely in a tense emotional state, regardless of its pitfalls.)

## The Other Way

An opposite type of clump, centered on an immensely enjoyable experience, demonstrates another manner for clumps to interact. Desirable clumps include sex, as in the example below, or any number of events such as hearing a song, growing a relationship, listening to a pleasant story, experiencing a religious awakening, and so on.

Suppose a man had sex with his wife. Their love is mutual and methods of intercourse afford maximum satisfaction providing a high rate of successful orgasm. The following diagram illustrates the clumps associated with lovemaking:

```
7             7             7             7             7
8  8  8  8  8  8  8  8  8  8  8  8  8  8  8  8  8  8  8
7  8  9  9  9  9  9  9  9  9  9  9  9  9  9  9  9  9  8
7  8  9   S  e  x   W  i  t  h   W  i  f  e  9  8  7
7  8  9  9  9  9  9  9  9  S  9  9  9  9  9  9  9  9  8
8  8  8  8  8  8  8  8  8  S  8  8  8  8  8  8  8  8  7
7             7             S             7             7
```

In this case, reaching tier seven means that he experiences a passing thought of sex. (I numbered the clumps for the larger numbers to be attracting.) When he reaches the sevens, his wife might respond positively, but this state in no way guarantees an orgasm. When reaching the nines, his wife makes physical contact; however, another constraint such as a crying child or the lack of a bed and privacy could still prevent reaching "Sex With Wife." In this diagram system S represents a near miss or last-minute exit path, including the crying child or privacy concerns, but it also includes the man falling asleep while waiting for his wife to come to bed, or even that he started to have intercourse with his wife, and then something went wrong in the early execution.

In the above example, some of the clumps strive for the preservation of sexual favors that the man currently receives. A seven clump might correspond to making himself pleasing to look at. An eight clump could be keeping her old boyfriend out of the picture. Clearly instability in these clumps leads to some dangerous behaviors. If, for example, his mate chose to discontinue the sexual relationship, the man would still reach tier eight and possibly tier nine, but be left with repeated and extreme frustration. These frustrations have to be dealt with, which normally means another set of predictably angry mental states. If these behaviors develop in desperation, then assume they will be of the more unstable variety, filled with violence and potentially debilitating mental frustration.

## Back to the Main Theme

What is the relationship between doublethink and clumps? Clumps are illogical, convoluted, confused, inconsistent, evolving, and deceitful, just like philosophy is. Where can you start to unravel the knot? With a direct logical approach? No! The human mind moves much too quickly. By the time the mind discovers a horrible clump, it starts building diversions around the mess.

Fear not, though, since there is another option; intentional doublethinking does not follow the normal rules of clumps behavior. If a mind says to avoid a certain idea or stimuli, doublethink selects the avoided area. If a clump designates a group of behaviors evil, doublethink calls them good. An intentional doublethinker destabilizes his thinking processes, and then a fresh group of clumps install and organize themselves. A committed, accepting doublethinker repeats the disruption again and again. Eventually the mind settles on a pattern of behavior more closely aligned to how the mind and its essential body interact with the world, actually improving stability and creating less misalignment. As a net result, the patterns of thinking grow more logical, more consistent, and more singlethink.

I cannot estimate the quantities and sizes of the clumps in a person's mind. Perhaps hundreds of very large and trillions of small ones constitute a mind? And surely there are infinite ways to combine them together. However, I feel fairly confident that a person who purposefully doublethinks only reorganizes a tiny portion of clumps at any one time.

As soon as the mangling occurs, an unstable situation arises. A person experiences some of the feelings the normal connections sought to avoid. Soon repairs reestablish the system. New clumps are formed quickly and attached to negative emotions, created for the purpose of avoiding the undesirable feelings stumbled into while doublethinking. At the same time, additional external stimuli continue to flow in. In other words, the old self combined with ongoing surroundings prove impossible to ignore. Thus, the remaining system of clumps and the surrounding environment limit intentional doublethink's destructive capabilities.

A person could, for example, doublethink until he or she was ready and able to place a hand on a hot stove. But then another memory of touching a hot metallic surface may suddenly reappear, which prevents the unfortunate event. But even if this pain-filled thought also fails, then the intense scorching sensation, the smell of burning flesh, and the subsequent trip to the hospital all tend create a new set of clumps, which will ultimately prevent future reoccurrences of intentionally touching burning hot things.

# 8 Directed Confusion:
## Take it Slowly

*The test of a first-rate intelligence is the ability to hold two opposed ideas in the mind at the same time, and still retain the ability to function.*

—F. SCOTT FITZGERALD

Confusion psychotherapy probes the mind to find the causes of anxiety and fear, and then it corrupts the thought processes associated with these clumps, allowing the mind to exorcize itself of the most awful, painful, recurring emotions. This chapter describes confusion psychotherapy and gives a short sample.

I encourage the reader to finish the entire book before attempting his or her own analysis. For better or worse, doublethink, combined with psychoanalytic techniques, strips away many mental barriers. Shortly thereafter, the mind replaces old barriers with new ones, almost as fast as doublethink destroys them. This preventative quality of clumps should stop a doublethink follower from committing all sorts of regrettable endeavors. Pain provides a powerful motive.

Under certain conditions, however, confusion psychotherapy could lead an individual to perform destructive, illegal, or cruel acts: Although I have experienced the benefits of these techniques, I fear for someone like "Gary." After a number of days of intentional doublethinking, Gary decided to commit suicide. Doublethink allowed Gary to consider putting a loaded gun inside his mouth and even removed all the normal mental obstacles preventing it. He overcame fear of death and fear of guns. He visualized the end of mental torture, seeing through the veil of religious rules and sin to be able to pull the trigger. His thoughts become uninhibited by those recently scrambled clumps that previously diverted him from this pattern of thought.

I reiterate: At this time I have no evidence that clumps reconstruct quickly enough to prevent disaster in all individuals, or even most individuals. Therefore, any who choose to practice this form of therapy are forewarned of the risk. I have conducted no studies and have only myself as a patient. When practicing this therapy, I always find myself in a confused mode of thinking—highly indecisive and disoriented. After the sessions my mind returns to most of the old habits. There seem to be a nearly infinite number of clumps that are impossible to destroy en mass. This trait of human behavior displays itself in all individuals via the existence of attributes like character, habits, integrity, and loyalty. The indestructibility of the attributes demonstrates the resilience found in systems of clumps.

On the positive side, confusion psychotherapy tends to cause a long-term calming effect. When overt doublethink blitzes the mind, thought patterns become more selective about what is worthy of anguishing over. The mind simply does not have the capacity to respond in the way it used to. Now the mind must evaluate when getting upset improves a situation. This evaluative process doesn't end when the patient finishes consciously thinking about doublethink but lingers on.

In essence, the confusion psychoanalytic method encourages dwelling on the most horrific thoughts in the human mind, and then trying to think about what could be worse.

Then say what is worse than worse, in order to make it seem real. Finally, state and believe the opposite; let everything look rosy. Repeat multiple times. When something terrible happens, take a mental note to bring it up later while intentionally doublethinking. If it really upsets, makes the whole body nervous, causes panic, anger, anxiety, and fear, then this pinpoints the most useful object to doublethink about. Visualize experiencing the biggest, most abominable nightmare, and ask how to make it even scarier—much scarier. Focus on the awful emotional pain associated with it. Then rapidly think of something pleasant, enjoyable.

In the upcoming example I follow the confusion psychoanalytic method. (One need not worry if the process bounces about in a disjointed manner. [Unpleasant clumps normally zig and zag all around.] The goal is not to map, understand, or organize them. Rather the objective is to experience the unpleasant clumps to destroy their disruptive nature. Once the mind no longer fears the attached jumbled mess that constitutes horrible memories, it thinks more efficiently.)

The driving habits of people in large cities particularly anger me:

> "I hate it when others become enraged when they drive. They pull up behind me, speeding beyond reason, honking, and flashing their headlights."

- *What would be worse?*

> "They ram into the back of my car, causing extensive damage, then they drive off. There is no accountability for their actions. They get away with this type of behavior, and nobody can stop them."

- *What makes me even angrier?*

> "I am traveling with a friend who exhibits these sorts of rude driving habits. I question his behavior. He says it is either "shit or be shit on." I sense that he thinks I am a fool, naive. I am disheartened because I made a plan for a kinder world—but the world treats me like shit!"

• *What would be worse?*

"I have really good ideas about people, but then everyone ignores me and ridicules me. I have put great energy into making my thoughts coherent and presentable. If friends and neighbors think I am stupid and annoying, then all is lost. It particularly frustrates me when nobody listens to my view. There should be a rule that says whenever someone is thoughtful, then everyone should respect him, or else our society merely promotes thoughtless irrational behavior."

• *Is there anything more upsetting?*

"The whole world works against me. Everybody thinks I am a fool. They all try to destroy me. I must prepare for the battle at all times, and plan to fight off all offenders to me. They attack me because they hate me. I am weak, so they think they can get me."

• *Name a more horrible outcome.*

"They physically attack me."

• *Say the opposite.*

"My children hug me. Strangers I meet trust me. Relatives listen and respect my opinion. The world grows kinder. Society confronts bad behaviors with police and jails. Inconsiderate thugs often face long prison sentences. I can win playing the cruel games of the world. I am an intimidating threat to those around me. Why do people try to hurt me? Why are they trying to get me? My best friends hate me, and I hate them. Tom ridicules the way I talk, even though I talk elegantly, indeed clearly. Tom picks me apart, despite my perfection."

• *What could be worse?*

"I am insignificant and vulnerable. I am one man against a nation of fools. I am small, but they are many. If a few people choose to gang up on me they can take me. They can destroy me. One strong man can overwhelm me. He will gain support of those around him. He intimidates his followers dominating the weak. I am a speck of dirt. I am king of the earth, emperor of the universe."

- *Think of a bigger fear.*

"He will torture and torment me. Others will find out what is inside of me. They see through my facade. I act like I am out for the world, but really I am out for me. If everyone knew how I felt they would banish and shun me. I have been found out. I am wrong—the people around me are very accepting, understanding of my point of view. Everybody loves confusion. Nobody wants to gang up on me or fix me. Candy, ice cream, sex, money, security. I have betrayed a friend by telling a secret about his future plans. I leaked it to the ones who could stop it. I am no longer worthy of his trust. When he finds out he will hate me. He will love me. He wants others to mistreat him. I did not betray him. I told a lie and hurt everybody…"

(Please note: *The fears above caused real anxiety during the process of writing them down, but the people in my life would certify that these fears bear only some resemblance to my everyday life. In other words, temporary clumps guide my thoughts in the above instances; afterwards, things return to a more ordinary and calmer pattern of behavior.*)

I have engaged in this type of psychoanalysis for the past several years. Over numerous sessions my mind has stabilized and gained focus. When no longer haunted by the absurd self-imposed penalties of previous painful experiences, my mind travels more freely. In addition, my thoughts tend to find clarity of purpose as well as simplicity in logic.

The ideal confusion psychotherapy never glosses over fear to achieve happy thoughts. Doublethink confronts horrible clumps in part by manipulating the mind. It disarms the blocking clumps when uncertainty arises, eventually forcing us to find out the content of the most dreaded clumps, ultimately so we can manage them in a more efficient manner. In many cases, the fear surrounding a bad clump becomes far worse than the clump itself. It helps to travel to the edge, such as going to the areas that cause the greatest anxiety, then tricking ourselves into crossing into the awful clumps associated with the ones that tell the mind to go back.

## Rational

If a person always avoids doublethink of all types, one might term his or her mind "rational." This "rational" mind attempts to achieve absolute order and consistency, but, in fact, never obtains perfection. Inevitably there exist fragments of nonsense and corruption, including memories of horrible clumps. Unfortunately the "rational" mind normally, and seemingly wisely, stops short of entering horrible clumps, and it never overcomes fear that may be totally irrational. This fear hems in the 'rational' mind with impenetrable boundaries. The 'rational' mind, in essence, imprisons itself with deceptive clumps. Ironically the mind wishing to maximize 'rational' thinking should instead use intentional doublethink to rid itself of tainted clumps.

# Freud: Reworking His Theories

*Consciousness deceives.*
*Consciousness is self-delusion.*
—TOR NORETTRANDERS, *THE USER ILLUSION*

Freud, the father of psychoanalysis, laid the groundwork for describing various types of mental functioning. Although his work ran into criticism from all corners, it held its own and endures; indeed, it permeates psychology even today. Thus the reader might ask what elements connect Freud's work to doublethink? What separates the two methods? What justifies yet more literature rehashing the father of psychoanalysis? This chapter compares several key features of the Freudian method, his with mine, roughly in each other's terms. Relying upon the psychological models of the previous chapters, I map Freud's work to concepts of doublethinking.

Freud was a dedicated scientist, and while a committed follower of the doublethink philosophy might question the need for this assumption, for the time being I give Freud the benefit of the doubt. I temporarily accept that human behavior is somewhat determined, and that empirical data predicts mental states and activities. In other words, I will use the scientific method trusted so dearly by Freud; that is, I will manipulate the clues of human actions to explain and predict our thought processes. I pick and choose only selected portions of Freud's work. Assume that the vast subject areas not referenced are either unnecessary for the purposes of this book or are inconsistent with my views.

For this discussion, Freudian psychoanalysis provides a benchmark. And despite the amazing things Freud was able to accomplish, I take issue with some of the theories and applications found in his basic methods. The doublethink philosophy models diverge from conventional psychoanalysis at its core; thus, it is appropriate to consider only the works of the most important figure in the beginning of this field, and let his followers, who built off his less than perfect system, be judged accordingly by those who wish to do so.

To better understand psychoanalysis, we need to clarify some of the terms Freud used and their relationship to the mental clumps detailed earlier in this book. The clump theories merge with and expand upon the various phenomena first systematized by Freud (I will liberally interpret Freud.) In fact, the doublethink method of confusion psychoanalysis parallels Freudian methods often, but only to a point. Understanding both the parallels and divergences, better explains how the mind functions, adding another useful dimension.

**Id:** In Freud's work the id (Hall [1954] 1999, 39) roughly describes the portion of the mind that provides a home to the basic functions. Sometimes it imitates the function of an autopilot that flies a plane in calm skies; other times it imitates a frog jumping away from a pursuing child.

The autopilot analogy corresponds to clumps that act with little emotion while decisively maneuvering the mind through lesser intermediate clumps. The id activities require limited consideration. Although autopilot id patterns may be complex and long in duration, they tend to be linear. For example, a person walking illustrates the id in action. His feet move with little thought, emotion, or debate. An experienced walker does not need to consider each step. The inputs are viewing the sidewalk, touching the ground, and remembering the neighborhood's layout. The function in this case is feet moving. Assuming the walker encounters the normally expected features throughout the trip, the id then directs the feet using almost no emotion or turmoil.

In the other extreme of the id behavior, it moves like a scared frog, acting decisively as well but with much emotion attached. Certain people jerk back with fright when touched unexpectedly, while others scream when they spot a mouse on the floor. It is sometimes referred to as reacting without thinking. The significant difference separating frog jumping from autopilot types of id behavior is the nervousness and anxiety attached to one but not the other. (After an unsettling event occurs, the mind often floods itself with measures to prevent it happening again. Anxiety-driven thoughts that consider multiple courses of actions and rules to prevent reoccurrence are no longer the id, but rather the ego and super ego.)

The above examples illustrate the two extremes (frog jumping and autopilot), but the key is to consider the common traits of id behavior. In clump terms, the id follows paths leading to a solution that ignores alternatives. The id exposes itself when the mind's behavior requires little thoughtful consideration during the execution of it actions. This, however, does not mean that the id cannot be trained. A great athlete, such as Michael Jordan, played basketball with an id conditioned by intensive practicing to produce graceful actions and feats of dexterity. His id executed through his body that famous athleticism. During games Michael did not debate each move of every finger, toe, and elbow for several seconds; instead, he laid out a course of action and allowed the id to follow through based on practice as well as incoming stimuli telling him where the defenders were moving to.

By similar means an engineer's id performs multiple mathematical calculations and comparisons with little emotion or turmoil. The engineer trains his id to manipulate scientific data. He sees the numbers 2 and 3 as $2 \times 3 = 6$, $3 + 2 = 5$, $2/3 = 0.666$, and $2 - 3 = -1$. He does not waste time deciding the sums and fractions; the id just supplies mathematical solutions the way Michael Jordan's id placed the ball into the hoop.

In Freud's model the id represents the desire for action, in some cases immediate gratification. In terms of clumps, the id specifically represents a condition where the input stimuli lead to an action with little consideration given to alternative responses. The id takes the least confusing or least dubious path. Non-id behavior includes complex relations of clumps that prevent lust-filled men from raping women on the street, stops hungry kids from cutting to the front of the cafeteria line, holds back upset sport fans from killing referees. These instances represent the lack of actions. Idleness in this case is the result of a debate occurring, as well as the presence of emotions to drive the debate in the first place. The potential rapist mentally compares life in prison to an orgasm. Hungry children measure the cost of getting caught and visiting the principle versus eating lunch five minutes sooner. And the football fan accepts a bad call in order to stay in the stadium for the second half. These evaluations demonstrate the ego in action, and are outside the capabilities of the id.

**Ego:** Freud's ego develops strategies for getting what the id wants in an efficient manner (Hall [1954] 1999, 41). The doublethink model equivalent is the navigation through the various clumps that consider and compare. A person's mind receives stimulation in some manner that causes a change in the current mental state to occur. This new state leads to another state and so on. Eventually the mind reaches an output that responds to the initial stimuli with an action. But when the ego guides, the mind passes through clumps that debate or allow for the consideration of two paths, or in other words, the ego doublethinks. The ego is doublethink in that it places emotional value on two or more diverging paths and follows them without acting until it can decide the superiority of one direction over the other. (By the way, this method has no set maximum time limit and no guarantee of success.) The ego in all cases considers options and attempts to gain the greatest good for the id, or the most pleasant stimuli.

Because our minds constantly evolve, when the first attempt at obtaining a goal results in failure, the setback modifies the clumps. If the goal is still desired, then a new updated clump attempts to reach the objective. When ultimately successful, the mind retains a memory of which course of action finally obtained a goal. In most cases, similar clumps lead to similar results; in other words, the ego can act empirically—and does. The ego remembers what happened the last ten times along with the details, and this information is used for predicting the future.

The ego says to a woman, "Don't have unprotected sex with a drug-addicted bisexual male," because it predicts the consequences of an evening frolic will result in a slow painful death. The ego fights for the future, even when that handsome heroin user is trying to seduce her, and she is really considering the fun of such hedonistic delights. The ego fights the id (libido in this case) since it predicts long-term pain followed by death as outweighing any temporary gain via sexual satisfaction.

Over time as the mind experiences this kind of decision making, its clumps evolve into greater complexity. The mind further increases the sophistication of its ego, often through activities such as going to school, reading books, and just living life. The ego processes ultimately develop a defined or planned path of clumps. When the ego discovers what it considers optimal and follows without further consideration, the resultant behavior is considered the id again. In other words, Michael Jordan's ego practiced and planned the moves, while his id executed the game-tying three-pointer. The electrical engineer's ego studied the potential current paths and combined with switching logic, while the id pushed the button that turned on the light bulb for the millionth time.

As Freud recognized, the id and ego fight with each other. The id attempts to find the most direct path—*now!* The ego slows the process and searches for the most efficient or optimum approach, even if it requires in-depth consideration. The ego is methodical and thoughtful, while the id is impatient.

**Super ego:** For Freud it represented a developed moral system, values, virtues, and so on. The super ego is in part passed along from parents to children. In some instances, parents reward and punish to instill the desired behavior in their young. In other cases heredity as well as miscellaneous factors influence the development of the super ego (Hall [1954] 1999, 46).

One of the most interesting aspects of Freud's super ego model is when it works for a goal with no benefit to the individual, or acts altruistically. Admittedly all these descriptions overly simplify the views of Freud, but the super ego essentially represents a philosophy or a guide to aid decision making that may go against what the id and ego desire.

In the clump model, the super ego represents the blockades that vigorously prevent the mind from traveling to other areas the ego and id would otherwise go to. When the mind experiences very bad or very good emotions, and attempts to repeat or avoid them, it either encourages entering of various clumps, or it closes down certain options. When the mind deliberately avoids clumps, Freud termed the behavior the super ego. Because of the anticipation of emotional and extremely painful clumps, the super ego locks out certain clumps as completely as possible. The super ego is stubborn; it often ignores the pleas of the impulsive id and logical ego. Indeed, the super ego defies logic in those cases where the ego's empirical, derived solutions are ignored.

If a father tells his son not to steal, then reinforces it with strong disciplined love, the boy forms clumps that discourage his mind from even thinking about breaking the rules. The phenomenon described by this example of Freud's super ego is simply explained by the mind closing down certain paths. The boy removes the option of stealing; he then reinforces the concept with barriers of clumps all steering far away from "bad" behavior. Eventually, when the obvious opportunity to shoplift arises, the boy will not comprehend a significant monetary benefit. His id wants the goods, while his ego knows it can take merchandise out the door with very low risk, but the super ego effectively circumvents the ability of stealing from occurring. Even when logic tells him he could get away with a crime and receive no punishment, his father's lingering teachings distort the clear view of the situation. Discontinuity arises between his behavior and the advantages at hand. He may have the opportunity to take thousands of dollars worth of electronics, but he fails to execute because in this instance the super ego encourages honesty and integrity.

But the super ego extends further and sadly lays the groundwork for some forms of mental illness. The super ego has the potential to go beyond what is sensible, or, in other words, confuse itself. A person's overactive super ego might, for example, limit behavior in ways that are not religious, practical, or beneficial to a person or the people around this person. This form of super ego behavior practically defines many mental illnesses, becoming too restrictive, hemming in behavior to the point that an individual lives a miserable existence.

In the clump model, the super ego normally comprises a more complex and confused thought pattern. The turmoil that exists in this area of the mind fills much of the first six chapters of this book. Once a person holds a certain view on behavior, and then reinforces it with sufficient discipline or other stimuli, the resultant clump pattern vigorously resists visiting of certain thoughts and memories. The mind erects a fortress around anything that questions the established rule against entering a "bad" clump. If the fortress becomes too large, powerful, mixed up, or unruly, a person's behavior turns bizarre. The mind loses continuity between incoming stimuli and outward actions. Sometimes this behavior appears extremely illogical and unconnected to the surrounding environment.

But do not get too carried away in the negative view either. The super ego phenomenon did explain generosity and altruism. The super ego is not required to bow to the ego and id, allowing it to do those deeds generally considered to be good: helping the poor, adopting disabled children, donating to colleges, and supporting political causes, just to name a few. The super ego denies the logic of the ego and the desires of the id, preventing the pursuit of selfish acts with narrow short-term benefits.

Regardless of whether or not the super ego ultimately helps more or hurts more, some could argue the ego is simply satisfying itself and that the super ego concept is not needed to complete the model. If this were the case, it fails to explain the super ego's baffling, erroneous actions. In other words, the ego only doublethinks by considering options, placing value on conflicting goals. The ego evaluates multiple paths, in some instances it daydreams and visualizes impossible situations. And the close companion to ego, the id, doublethinks out of stupidity, poor comprehension, or inability. The id by itself is hedonistic, foolish, and shortsighted. But the super ego doublethinks in a whole other league. The super ego flat out lies. The super ego defies logic, examining the input stimuli and then intentionally ignoring optimal solutions.

As a whole Freud's id, ego, and super ego concept can be replaced by clumps and physical inputs to the mind. The mind continuously receives excitations and decides which to react to, enhance, or ignore. Those reactions requiring little debate constitute the id, the more considered clumps the ego, and the most stubborn ones the super ego.

**Repression/suppression:** A manifestation related to the id, ego, and super ego (Hall [1954] 1999, 85). In the clump model, for example, a homophobic's id might have a desire for a homosexual relationship, but the super ego represses this desire. Close physical contact with a person of the same sex could awaken the ego's paths to dangerous feelings. In various circumstances, acknowledgment of homosexual passions causes great anxiety and fear. A fortress surrounds the repressed gay notion. To keep the gay fantasies hidden, extreme levels of emotion attach to the protecting barriers. Whenever the ego wonders too closely to the homosexual excitement, it recoils with raw anger and panic. Most likely the mind overreacts beyond that justified by reentering the core feared vision or action. The protecting super ego emotions tell us it is best to skip the subject altogether.

Consider the act of two guys kissing intimately. Assume Tom dreads that he may accidentally become romantically involved with another man. Being aware of the tremendous social consequences of conducting himself in such a manner, he nervously avoids anything that comes remotely close to arousal. Tom fights violently to avoid exposing himself to images that bring him into the realm of thinking about sexual voyeurism (like a man sweetly seducing a man). He responds with reactions totally out of proportion to the incoming stimuli present, mocking other males who are not as masculine, seeking to discourage anyone from thinking he is capable of being excited by a queer. The logic of this behavior escapes those around Tom.

If Tom is somehow tricked or confused into crossing these barriers, he may respond violently to ensure the repressed clump never exposes itself again. Or he could enter the repressed area with tremendous joy, excitement, and relief at finding the homosexual actions cause little pain and are really very fun. He may later recover from a lapse to rebuild the walls protecting against the gay orientation in hopes of removing himself from the shame of this alternative lifestyle.

In terms of doublethink, it is essential to split repression concepts into two categories. One group is repressed/suppressed overtly, and the other is done so out of a lack of interest. Various clumps are avoided, and some are simply too weakly connected to others or external stimulation to ever get called up.

A recipe for a type of soup that tastes bland falls into the category of low interest. The mind has little incentive to prepare a soup with limited flavor, thus, it tends to forget the steps of preparation. In this case, a memory mostly detaches. Later on, if the person who forgot the recipe was dining at a friend's house and was served a bowl of meat, noodles, and broth prepared a certain way, it might spark a recall. But since there is so little interest, the soup recipe may also simply lie in the background unnoticed. One could possibly retrieve the recipe from deep recesses, but it would take an added effort to overcome the lack of enthusiasm.

The first type of repression/suppression (homosexuality in my example) received all the interest from Freud. In the overtly repressed memory, the mind encircles undesirable clumps, intentionally avoiding them by the use of still other clumps, which prevents the mind from reaching the core "bad" ones. Then there are additional layers added to protect the mind from the barrier clumps as well. There are many ways to break down repressions, but the fact that they exist provided Freud with much of his material.

He sought means for building passages through the walls partitioning our mind. In this quest I think Freud was a little too ambitious, going beyond his knowledge of the functioning mental processes. He continuously looked for repression but did not really understand the mechanics of how it worked. When he talked about the Oedipus complex and castration, he drew out strong emotions and assumed he found a well-spring of repression. Contrary to Freud I think carrying out extended conversations about sleeping with your mother, killing your father, and lopping off your genitals is bound to bring out strong emotions—with or without repression. Having said all that, it probably is still beneficial for a person to experience the strong emotions Freud tapped into. These overreactions and insecurities are at the core and near other clumps containing repressed memories. Thus, while he was logically way off base with the rationale for some of his theories, he likely succeeded to some extent in spite of his mistakes. Reaching near the source of corrupted thought patterns prepared his patients to overcome great fears. Although the patients were misled, they also became adept at confronting irrational anxiety, and grew less intimidated by many of their false barrier clumps. The patients likely found more efficient systems for dealing with emotions and stimuli. (Note the similarities to confusion psychoanalysis.)

And this brings us to a very important point: The mind has many areas it does not want us to visit and purposely blocks the paths. How can we logically convince ourselves to violate our own barrier clumps? Could we specifically tell ourselves to activate the memories and thoughts we do not want to see? Or should we trick our brains on purpose? Once we reach the forbidden locations, changes occur, mostly to a more robust and more stable state. Our barrier clumps are broken down, and our emotions are now more closely aligned with our physical needs.

The super ego consists of steel bars and barbed-wire fences the ego logically respects, in most cases to avoid bad emotions. Exposing the ego to gross illogic confuses it to the point where it can no longer distinguish between which clumps cause negative feelings and which do not (it stops following the subjective right and wrong imposed by the super ego). The ego loses its boundaries. The purposeful doublethinking mind meanders about from clump to clump not knowing what it will find. Once the steel bars are broken down and the wire cut, the penetrated mind finds out the obstacles were poorly placed, and then concludes that the super ego should not be trusted in many cases.

Throughout most of this book, I try to expose you to clumps to which you would not ordinarily go. Maybe that is all I do, and this really is what Freud strove for as well. (Strangely, Freud's bizarre explanations parallel doublethink; the odder his reasons for our most intimate thoughts, the more disruptive talking about them seems to be to a misguided super ego.)

**Sex:** Freud clearly recognized a strong connection between sex and the activities of the human mind, but his explanations were contrived and cumbersome. The clump model explains sex in a much more straightforward manner. The clump model describes sex as an activity with the ability to create extremely high levels of stimulation, often pleasant. These stimuli of course center around the various obvious organs identified by Freud. Because of the potential for the repetition of intense pleasure, our minds act in unusual ways: Become obsessed with the stimulation of a penis, for example. We get confused and overwhelmed with religious constraints on sex, tricked out of getting intimate because of complex social limitations, and on and on.

Due to extreme levels of feelings involved, thoughts of sex often frustrate the mind—for example, by forcing it to entertain thoughts about breasts and vaginas, but then having a new relationship fail to reach the ultimate goal. The emotionally intense nature of a pleasurable sexual encounter explains the unusual behavior associated with someone who is not successful. Intense anxiety tends to rearrange clumps while in a state of desperation. Not surprisingly the clumps get loopy. The mind *very often* wants sex more than logic.

The doublethink model more or less shows consistency with the great significance of the sexual role for understanding human behavior that Freud put forward. Both methods acknowledge the importance of sex and its ability to disrupt mental soundness.

**Subconscious:** Freud recognized the existence and significance of the subconscious, but quite frankly he had limited comprehension regarding the details of its operation. There are now better explanations to which to attribute mental activities than the catchall dynamic subconscious Freud created. (Activities of the brain that are not conscious are by default subconscious. There are some functions such as regulating body temperature and hormonal releases, which are interesting, though outside the scope of this book. I will focus only on some portions of the subconscious activities Freud discussed in depth.) In the clump model the subconscious consists of different phenomena including these two key types:

1. Memory
2. Barrier and attracting clumps' connections to memory.

**Memory:** In terms of the subconscious, a memory is a clump a person is not in, but can still return to, such as previous visions, smells, and lusts. Memories retain ties to other clumps; that is when the right conditions of inputs and stimuli appear, related thoughts and images are recalled. Since memories are attached to other clumps, memories seem to lie in the background without completely disappearing. In my model, this type of subconscious is made up of memories accessed by activity in a nearby clump, an external physical stimuli, or internal stimuli.

**Barrier and attracting clumps**: A barrier clump directs the mind away from another clump. The mind encounters a set of stimuli and recognizes a problem. The mind does not need to examine every detail and possible outcome. It simply steers away from undesirable outcomes.

A grocery shopper picking fruit sees a pile of apples. She ignores the bruised ones and selects smooth red ones. Barrier clumps direct the shopper elsewhere avoiding thoughts of brown spots and spoilage. If the barrier clump was not there, the shopper would have either purchased the rotten apples and had them decay in the refrigerator, or she would have spent several seconds in thought regarding a whole series of events involving fruit spoilage. This is considered subconscious thought since the mind, if it needed to, would recall a number of memories and evaluate what is best to do. To illustrate the existence of the subconscious, assume all the apples were bruised and the shopper really wanted some anyway. Under these conditions, the previously subconscious memories are recalled and put into action. The shopper estimates the rate of deterioration, the actual number of fruit needed until a return grocery store trip, and which apples have the smallest nicks and cuts. She opens up the subconscious thought process and reviews the contents.

Barrier clumps have the ability of preventing entry into unpleasant or unneeded thoughts. Barrier clumps demonstrate the existence of subconscious clumps because the mind acts based on memories that need not be recalled. The mind summarizes and represses memories in the name of efficiency and avoiding pain.

The inverse, or attracting, clump is the clump that when active causes the mind to follow a defined path toward a desired state. When a man sees a sexy woman and feels a bulge in his jeans, he responds subconsciously. The attracting clump escorts the mind directly to a sexual fantasyland. The mind does not need to weigh all the consequences of inappropriate behavior. The man and his groin remember a similar pleasant experience, perhaps buried away, and decide to go directly there. This is subconscious, because the mind's behavior is based on memories. The mind connects a vision of a short skirt to erection, and even ejaculation. Similar to the barrier clump, a whole series of thoughts are glossed over by the attracting clump. The mind keeps dormant many memory clumps, while just a few key paths navigate the activities toward desired goals.

The subconscious memories can keep the mind on a narrow path. If the man filled with thoughts of infidelity gets into the presently subconscious religious memories, he risks losing pleasure. Thus, his lusty thoughts craftily avoid all memories of religion; instead they direct the mind to pleasure fulfillment. In this case, the morality type subconscious clumps are held at bay.

Looking at all the aspects of the clump subconscious model, we see that it is really not a separate little mind scheming and performing tasks independently; rather, it is a series of clumps optimized to perform in certain ways. The logic remains obscured (but potentially able to be recalled). The mind skips along on the surface only briefly touching various clumps on its journey.

**Freudian slip:** Using a phrase or word inappropriately often revealing a person's true feelings. Once again the phenomenon unquestionably occurs, but the explanation provided by Freud lacks credibility. In the clump method a verbal misstep indicates a failed attempt to block a clump. A person did not want to think or say something, but allowed a path unprotected very near the naughty thought. A person may not want to say the word fat for fear it would offend a large friend. During a discussion the word rat is about to be spoken. The person who is talking about rats may say "fat" inadvertently, because the clumps for articulating both words lie very close to each other. More precisely, the ability to blockade a thought from being verbalized was unsuccessful because an indirect path to the "bad" fat clump was stumbled upon. The word fat forms a clump similar to rat. The mind accepted an approximate recall for rat—fat.

The clump explanation also allows for instances when slips contain unstated desires. In the above example, ineffectively barricaded desire clumps could have motivated the person to wish to make an issue of her friend's weight. Perhaps she found the weight of a friend made her feel better about her own large body, and one of her clumps wanted to focus attention on how much better she looked than her huge friend. Generally a pleasant conversation requires that a person block clumps that would anger the other members of the group. (In part, having the wrong clump active to avoid it further increases the likelihood of its misuse since clumps are closely connected when active.)

Contrary to Freud, however, another motivation for the slip may include a desire to move quickly to a complete spoken thought. Certainly it would create considerable frustration to dwell on every word of every sentence for several minutes, to ensure one never said something offensive or incorrectly. To save time in this case the mind may see an approximate clump match and assumes a correlation exists when it does not. Thus the mind appears intentionally inconsistent with the rules of conversing, when in fact it was only lazy in the execution, with no other hidden agenda. Perhaps Freud was not sloppy enough himself to recognize the prevalence of this phenomenon. Again Freud's scheming and underhanded subconscious appears a bit silly. There just seems to be better explanations.

**Dreams:** Freud called dreams "the royal road to a knowledge of the unconscious" (Freud [1900] 1991, 2). The doublethink model differs significantly from Freud's explanations on this matter. To make sense of dreams with respect to doublethink, one must first build on the previous subconscious concept. Again, it consists of a group of clumps that are not active. They lie dormant for two reasons:

1. They are protected from activation by other barrier clumps.
2. There is simply a lack of interest, or connections, to clumps that are active.

*(In addition locations in pockets of the mind can be partially active and partially blocked. This happens especially in large clumps, which consist of groups of smaller clumps. A large clump may detach from some of its constituent memories, actions, and logic, causing a portion of the mind to become inactive. These partially severed mini clumps may stand by for duty. Proximity determines the active areas, that is, the relevance of these things the mind is not currently doing but could do.)*

As Freud discovered, dreams penetrate subconscious clumps, but to understand why, it is necessary to back up again. The basic purpose of clumps is to respond to stimuli and control future stimuli. For example, a feeling of coldness causes a series of thoughts that often lead to putting a blanket on. Our mental states and physical actions are in large part ruled by outside stimulation. Coldness activates a series of clumps to relieve that unpleasant chill. But what happens when a person sleeps? The incoming stimuli and outgoing signals from the brain alter dramatically (most likely related to biochemical reasons that go well beyond my personal knowledge). Many of the mind's clumps are still present, but major rules of clump interactions change. All the structures of an awake person mutate and distort during resting periods.

The cold sensation coming into the brain no longer serves the same function. A dream scenario could be as follows: Cold is the input stimulation. A person dreams about an incident at work from the previous day. The coldness tells the person to put on a sweater. Searching for the sweater causes a panic because a wild animal in the closet tugs on it. Relief is found since the animal turns out to be the sleeper's cat, which only wants to play. Next the dreamer visits to the cold food section at the grocery store....

The key in this example is not holding the mind accountable in a dream to the same requirements as it is when awake. One cannot expect a sleeping person to get out of bed, retrieve the needed blanket, and remain sleeping. During a dream the rules change.

Now generalize and assume that virtually all the clumps change while people sleep; one would expect the mind to run through many sorts of ideas, visions, and memories in a haphazard fashion. If the thoughts make little sense, who cares? The mind concedes there are limited responses to stimuli. So whatever thinking processes and physical actions occur they do not need to resolve actual stimulation. (They cannot do much of anything anyway, so why make the effort?) Essentially the dreaming mind rambles about in a state of anarchy.

The normal protocols no longer apply, thereby establishing an explanation for dream content making so little sense. Dreams don't have to adjust or account for the negative consequences of their actions; therefore, the sleep clumps just sort of bounce about in all sorts of absurdities. Logic and coherence are not inherent to clumps. Sleep frees the mind to consider whatever nonsense its liberated, confused thoughts lead it to. Yet some structure remains in dreams to allow visions and other types of memories. Nightmares sometimes repeat, also indicating additional structure. (Perhaps other patterns will emerge with more study. Many potential characteristics of these activities remain interesting but unfortunately exceed my understanding at this point.)

Freud had other ideas; he claimed dreams are a type of wish-fulfillment (Hall [1954] 1999, 25). This was an unfortunate assumption. Yes, dreams are clumps, and clumps help obtain what is desired in an awake person. But when a person sleeps, the clumps are utterly useless in delivering almost anything significant in terms of wish-fulfillment. (I am ignoring basic life-sustaining functions of the brain such as heart beating and breathing.) Additionally, the clumps are not held accountable, nor are they expected to work, play, or solve calculus problems. Therefore, searching for a wish in a dream approximates looking for rhyming words in shredded newspaper. Yes, there are rhyming words in the scraps of paper, and yes, there are patterns to be found by looking, but it would be extremely difficult to piece back together little strips of the Sunday *Chicago Tribune*, and looking for words with the same sounding endings only confuses the issue.

Despite Freud's over-reliance on wish-fulfillment, one should not underestimate the significance of his dream work. During the state of dreaming, the mind goes to places ordinarily restricted. Since the confused mind follows few discernible rules, it inevitably stumbles into clumps that are blocked when awake. The mind discovers unconscious places (barricaded thoughts and associated emotions). It locates memories and ideas that are inaccessible and protected while awake. Analyzing dreams after the fact, as Freud revealed, allows a person to penetrate those areas of the mind that hide.

In many cases the asleep mind travels far into clumps that the awakened mind restricts with fear, anger, and guilt. A person avoids awkward social situations, but finds while sleeping a visual image and the associated panic that results from walking into a crowd naked. The mind seems to realize its nightly freedom and uses this time go willy nilly about in all sorts of clumps. It comprehends that logic as well as consistency have very limited value. In the dream state, a person changes into someone else, travels to distant lands instantaneously, and revives dead people from the other world. While asleep, the mind follows fewer sensible rules. Contrast this with the awake state when incoming stimuli need meaningful responses to guide our actions to desirable types of stimulation, or at least to avoid the certain unpleasantries.

**Nightmare:** A nightmare to Freud was a complicated affair that I do not see the need to go into here. For the clump model, nasty dreams result from the mind entering an area normally protected while awake. This unearthed clump creates undesirable stimuli, but because of loosened nocturnal rules, the mind allows for its occurrence. Nightmares are most likely loosely linked, as Freud believed, to an unpleasant event. That event drove the mind to create barriers and secondary barriers with horrible emotions attached to them, all of which prevent the awake person from having to relive the direct thoughts and emotions that are associated with an unpleasant event. While sleeping, however, the dreaming mind penetrates the secondary clumps, or barriers. The dreamer comes dangerously close to having to deal with what it utterly believes constitutes the most awful thoughts. The dreamer uses any means available to prevent him- or herself from reaching that frightful destination.

The puzzling question that arises is why the mind allows all sorts of unusual clump patterns, but then panics at certain times. For some reason, nightmare-type fears transcend sleep and are partially addressed while a person dreams. It appears the mind normally places high priority on sleep as well as relative calm during the night. But it also retains the ability to react to severe situations and is willing to give up peace and contentment to prevent the entering of these unusually painful clumps. The scary dream about an ugly monster is similar to the act of waking up for loud noises, such as a smoke detector. In both cases, the mind retains the option of coming out of the dream state to a startled state.

*(I have observed that I frequently have a very slight nightmare in the morning when it is time to wake. It seems my mind somehow manipulates the dream pattern, making a little excitement to jar me free and get me ready to start the day.)*

## The Bigger Picture

From the confusion psychoanalysis perspective, it helps to confront the most awful nightmare day or night. Thus a person overcomes his or her fears and gets on with life. It is probably not terribly critical that anybody ever understands the exact root cause, but rather they penetrate the significant irrational fears as the abominations present themselves. It ultimately serves the purpose of mental stability to challenge the clumps of thoughts that scare the mind from exposing itself to the unthinkable. The unthinkable we know is usually not so bad.

Consider the obvious correlation between intentional doublethink and dreams. During dreaming the mind lets loose to indulge in many absurdities, with far fewer constraints than when awake. Afterward the mind recovers, relaxed and desensitized. The sleeper sees many scrambled memories during the dream state. Dreaming is also a time when we posses limited emotions, and correspondingly construct few new barriers. The mind experiences strange events while not reacting very strongly. (Amazingly people can remain asleep through the night.)

It seems that sleeping permits oddly configured clumps to activate in the desensitized mind. The mind bombards itself with absurd ideas that bewilder and then numb the mind. In this state, the strings that normally cause anxiety when conscious are cut and allow less to happen emotionally. Consequently, the sleeper calms down because the lack of response tells the mind it is okay to think about various painful subjects, thus allowing the individual to get closer to problem areas of their lives in a relatively pleasant manner.

As Freud discovered, during sleep the mind finds it can go into areas too difficult to consider during awake periods, and then amazingly in the morning the dreams are mostly forgotten. In addition, common experience recognizes the well-rested mind as fresh and clear, thinking openly about ideas that were too difficult the night before. The advice given for making a difficult decision often contains *sleeping on it*, followed by a review in the morning.

Indeed, I am convinced that one of the main purposes of dreaming is to obtain the identical outcomes as intentional doublethink. In both cases, the mind overwhelms itself with absurd ideas. The mind then desensitizes, allowing for the consideration of issues more freely. Forced doublethink purges extreme emotional overreactions and lesser emotions too. The doublethink-distracted mind releases itself from bondage to consider difficult and painful issues without the all the fear formerly associated with these traumatic memories. In this respect, free association, dreaming, and doublethink are all one in the same, that is, the mind's normal awake methods of operating cease. Clumps representing mere ramblings are activated. Doublethink, dreaming, and free association all offer means for passing all sorts of intentionally avoided ideas through the mind.

To once again return to Freudian terms, the super ego must be controlled. Doublethink, dreaming, and free association all attempt to break down the super ego. The super ego creates all sorts of illogical rules. In addition, the super ego stubbornly dictates behavior. Left unchecked, it would eventually lead to insanity. Fortunately, invading the areas protected by the super ego weakens its reign.

**Free association**: The term is a misnomer. Free only means that you reduce restrictions on your thought patterns. You allow yourself to experience thoughts in a manner you are not accustomed to. Freudian free association remains passive in the sense that all thoughts offer potential keys to unlocking the secrets inside the mind. A psychoanalyst allows the patient to ramble in most any direction, until something upsetting or distasteful occurs. Presumably the psychoanalyst asks the person lying on the couch to expound upon those items. The psychoanalyst tries to keep the person suspended in a state of judgment about his or her thoughts (Freud [1900] 1999, 87). In terms of clumps, Freud assumed the construction of a bad clump necessarily left it attached. In other words, if a horrible memory arose, and it created more unpleasant feelings, this chain of events remained linked. Thus the patient should try to follow each link in the chain back to the original memory of a root bad stimulus.

No evidence demonstrates, however, that interlocking intermediate steps must remain intact, and even if it did, there is no need to follow it back piece by piece. I diverge sharply from Freud here. In confusion psychoanalysis, once the patient finds the objects that are sensitive to him- or herself, he or she then focuses all energy on disrupting normal thought process on these very objects. The patient should purposefully express the opposite of what he or she thinks, intentionally pointing the process to the precise and exact reverse direction of where the ordinary clump directs it to go.

The advantage of doublethink comes from not allowing the patient the opportunity to avoid issues. In traditional free association, the mind is given the chance to find paths that circumvent the whole process. Freud's methods essentially meander from clump to clump, occasionally tricking the mind into going to a location it does not want to go to, sometimes stumbling onto the hot spot and causing cathartic experiences.

In confusion psychoanalysis, the subject specifically attacks the obstacles that prevent his or her mind from getting to the various painful thoughts. If a person focuses on areas that are upsetting and breaks down the barriers to getting to problematic memories and feelings, he or she will ultimately improve his or her ability to deal with difficult mental states. (When I use this method, I inevitably experience catharsis more quickly, more often, and more efficiently than any other method I've tried.)

Freud would not dispute the significance of painful irrational behavior, but he did use a significantly different method to attack it. If a psychological problem were a ten-story building, Freud sets the patient on top of it with a blindfold and box of dynamite. The patient's job entails getting to the basement and blowing the building up. By contrast, in doublethink he or she gets a giant crane, complete with a wrecking ball to bash away.

Freud's method in theory demonstrates more precision and elegance, but in practice it proves difficult to execute. Doublethink, although messier in theory, is much easier to perform. Just start knocking an iron weight against the side of the building until it collapses. In fact, doublethink consists of driving down the street hitting all problems with the wrecking ball. Freud, on the other hand, would have the patient going into each new building with a new packet of dynamite. If the patient developed only enough skill to blow up one building a month, newly constructed buildings could rise quicker still.

Admittedly the rebuilding of undesirable clump configurations presents a problem for doublethink, as it did for Freud. While doublethink is quicker, it is not perfect. Under ordinary circumstances clump manipulation provides a full-time job for the mind. Thinking that one can jump in the middle of the mix to extract all the troubled clumps assumes a bit too much of any of the confusion or psychoanalytic processes in general. The mind controls the clumps to its liking, ignoring common sense and taking itself where it wants to go.

In Freud's method, free associations often detour to prevent the mind from seeing its real problems. The mind allows only limited priority to finding its way back to sources of conflict. It disturbs people to see the mess. Their minds frequently attempt to simplify and make life easier, normally accepting the appearance of order to avoid the painful thoughts associated with disorder. They seek to smooth over problems and not root them out.

The benefit of intentionally confusing the clump system with doublethink stems from the process of the mind used to sort good ideas from the bad ones. The way the mind accomplishes sorting was already explained in earlier chapters, basically selection based on emotions. That is, options causing good emotions, or fewer bad feelings, are the ones held on to and carried through. Unfortunately, the mind sometimes fools itself. If an idea appears too painful but needs consideration, the mind can drop it, regardless of the later consequences. The mind frequently deceives itself out of fear of unpleasant thoughts. It avoids difficult clumps due to laziness in dealing with emotions. (Or instead of laziness, one could say the mind is conserving its resources for emergencies or for future anxiety that cannot be avoided.)

The weakness with Freudian psychoanalysis derives from the mind quickly finding an escape route around the troubled areas. Freud relied on the mind informing itself of the correct reason for dismissing ideas, but frequently the mind calls painful ideas absurd, stupid, nonsense, blasphemous, and so on. It troubles a person to know when he or she lies to him- or herself; the mind avoids the agony (of admitting to lying) by throwing itself off the track with words like crazy and foolish, effectively reducing the likelihood of immediately growing upset.

The advantage of intentional doublethink derives from confusing the mind into confronting specific areas it seeks to avoid. Just as doublethink cuts through philosophical beliefs, it also cuts through other mental barriers as well. Super ego rules run deep, creating painful clumps based on emotions and feelings that are even more deeply entrenched and difficult to consider. Doublethink cuts closer to the heart of the matter. Doublethink in some cases achieves what free association finds most difficult to do, disrupting rigidly held clump patterns and discouraging the mind from returning to old habits.

An effective approach to resolving poorly applied clumps uses some traditional psychoanalysis, as well as intentional doublethink. Traditional psychoanalysis establishes the structure, like a person wanting to confront a problem with alcoholism. From traditional psychoanalysis, "Henry" knows that his cruel father still lingers inside of his head. Now enters doublethink. The statements that follow are of the type that will cause a deeper understanding of what the intentional doublethinker has controlling the mind.

"My father was a cruel gentleman. I hate him, but love him too. He is both thoughtful and kind. He is good. I'm so afraid of him. He scares me, but I am not afraid of him. He is rotten…genuine. He treated my sisters so well sometimes, while beating them frequently. He is a bastard saint. I love the man I hate. I could kill him. I am afraid of him and his beautiful life."

*(The sentences above are highly condensed representation of what happens in "Henry's" mind; many emotions, visions, and memories are dredged up during such a process. I intentionally kept the verbiage short and concise to trick the mind, since this usually works better for me. When reading these, your mind needs to fill with images. So digest them slowly at first, allowing a group of related mental images to form, then quickly move to the next item. Repeat, repeat, repeat…. Finally, and very importantly, customize it for your own needs.)*

As this process continues, the emotional barriers start to crack. Henry's mind starts to lose the structure that holds the problem inside. Conflicting ideas trick him into unusual thought patterns. Emotionally Henry loses his sense of right and wrong, disorienting his values to the point where the unspoken speaks. Hearing one's self say the awful, exposes what really hides inside. He continues:

"My father never loved me. I loved him. He loved me, but I was not worthy of it. There was something distasteful about me. I am good and afraid. I am bad. I am honorable. I'm awful. Nobody loves me. Everybody loves me. Why should I try? I'm not the kind of person people want to be around. I am wonderful, strong, and fearless"

After completing several extended sessions such as this, Henry would likely find his super ego reigned in. He would be freer in his thoughts regarding his father. Henry would experience memories of his father with less emotional recoiling and angst.

Unfortunately some caution should be kept in mind. The combination of doublethink with psychoanalysis has proven extremely potent to me personally. Please treat it as such. I suspect that if it is not used with a great deal of care, it may lead an individual to an anxious super ego instead of a peaceful one. *(Thus far my test sample size has been limited to one.)*

## Mental Illness

Though I am not a serious student of mental illnesses, I have recognized some ailments seem to lend themselves to the doublethink clump model descriptions. I hope further study of clumps will provide useful information on mental illness.

**Depression:** It is the prevention of a person reaching clumps with significant pleasure in them. A person may, for example, believe certain clumps cause short-term elation, excitement, followed by extended periods of withdrawal from the source. Correctly assessing the situation or not, the person's barrier clumps avoid behavior containing enjoyment. The depressed individual systematically closes down those clumps that create energetic actions.

**Catatonic states:** Demonstrate a mind systematically preventing the amplification of multiple stimuli and/or avoiding those clumps surrounding stimuli amplification. The clump system effectively limits stimulation's impact and the corresponding normal responses.

**Phobias:** Consist of fears that the mind built a wall of more fear clumps around. A woman fears snakes. In addition to this fear, she also avoids caves and rocks since snakes live there. Phobias confuse because an unpleasant event may not reside in a fear clump that is the phobia. A phobia could be caves, caused by another phobia for snakes. The snake phobia can be a barricaded place around another different clump. This clump could also be a barrier to yet another clump. The ultimate root cause of the phobia could remain undetectable.

Phobias appear very irrational because the fear, which disrupts one's life, frequently bears little resemblance to something physically harmful.

**Repetitive behavior illnesses**: A series of clumps that repeat themselves the way a record skips. Clump A leads to B to C and finally back to A. Repetitive behavior is a confused, unpleasant logical system based on illogical assumptions similar to ordinary behavior, except that the term repetitive illness implies a disruptive element, caused by doing the same tasks over and over. The repetition brings no overall improvement in stimulation and creates great anxiety when the victim fails to perform tasks multiple times.

# 10 Doublethink Free Association: Breaking Apart the Mind

*We are not creatures of logic.*
*We are creatures of emotion.*
*Our logic is like a birch-bark canoe tossed*
*about on a deep, dark, stormy sea of emotion.*
—DALE CARNEGIE, *HOW TO STOP WORRYING*
*AND START LIVING*

The following is an example a free association formation—sort of rambling in an area I happen to know is sensitive to me. Then I unleash intentional doublethink and tears come to my eyes. I see the confusion, perhaps the wickedness of my soul combined with more confusion. I succeed in stirring the pot. It then settles back again, but I see glimpses of what lurks inside of my mind, what guides me.

"Why am I afraid of what others think about me? I do not care if they all find me stupid, foolish, obnoxious, or poorly dressed. I do care that they harbor these thoughts of me. I search for reasons and any other means to make them judge me wise, like writing books of philosophy. I know that some strangers will look at me and immediately try to make me out as inferior. They sense that I am made unstable by this sort of judgment. They toy with me, abusing my sincerity.

They mock me and the way I slur my s's. They laugh at me, thinking of me as little more than a silly fool.

"I should not become paranoid now, but also not be naive and ignore the behavior of those that mock me. I will instead overcome this fear of failure, while I tremble at the thought of not gaining the acceptance of others. Growing up, I often imagined that other people did not like me, or at least that's how some acted.

"I think everybody adores me; everybody hates me. They all want to spend time with me, getting to know the books I read, hobbies I enjoy, my children, and the engineering tasks I perform during the day. They all want to visit with their other friends. They all tease me because of my distracted mind and growing waistline. They all admire me for the way I solve construction problems around the house. I do care what my coworkers say about my errors and do not mind if they ridicule and belittle my ideas for better equipment. They can manipulate me to work long hours on useless tasks, but I am free to come home whenever I like—and quit as well. They find ways that to hurt me, by denying me promotions and pay raises. They wish to help me reach my highest goals and greatest happiness, with lots of money. They intimidate me with their high positions and expensive cars. They follow my lead and do as I command.

"I am free of the horror of being fired. It overwhelms me to think of working until I'm eighty because social security is no longer there. I think the government likes wage earners like me, and the accountants running it hate us. I loathe the idiotic bureaucrats, yet strangely I must admit I like their invisibility a great deal. My whole life is for pleasing the people I meet each day, each one trying always to please me. I am trapped in box of mixed-up anxiety. I am free; I am free. The knotted ropes inside my brain, bind me up and keep me from taking care of myself. I can do as I want and know this is so. The cruel people in the taverns hurt me so much when they deny me affection. I need to know they care as they order another round and tell the same stories about drinking too much over and over. The fact that alcoholics empathize does not affect me in any way. They are black- and brown-fanged monsters. I need their loving support to tell me that I am not a fool, mistakenly looking too closely at life. I cannot live without companionship of the people I so despise. They, on the other hand, beg me for my presence. I could care less what they think of me but would like them to worship my principles. But others could never say great things about me; that is juvenile and misguided. But that is how I really feel. I want them to serve me. Flatter me. Make me their king. I want to be despised, trampled on. I want my emotions ignored, and them to hurt me.

"Even now my mind tries to trivialize these feelings, holding back on feelings looking to break loose and express themselves. It knows where it is all going, my mind sensitizes to these key issues of the odd people I choose to interact with. It focuses in on the problem of not having enough money for a new car. I cannot hide from my greedy little existence, not caring about the starving kids I witness on the evening news. I am human. Fools like me can hide inside a protective barrier, preventing all but tranquil thoughts of jelly beans and guillotines. I can't overcome this constant anxiety but feel fine all the time. The path is hard and filled with thorny bushes and grizzly bears picking raspberries. It is easy to follow the road to success and advancement. All that was clear becomes spaghetti mixed with alphabet soup with rice. The whole world looks at me with a painful grin of contempt and elation. It all makes sense. What is inside of me is chaos in perfect order.

"I do not treat people badly. I treat them awfully. I am not worthy of others' admiration and do not work hard to achieve it. I want it all for myself, seeking opportunities to give my body to the cause of others.

"I am writing this book to gain the intellectual admiration of others. I could give a f—- what they think of me. I want them all to love me, but they can never love me. They think I am insane and the most competent mind of all time. I am a genius but very stupid, and they can clearly see it. I want them to love me as they lose their admiration, hurting me with their unkindness. I displease them, so they hurt me, kiss me, even worship me. They fight to give me praise. I despise them for liking me too much while they try to kill me. I cannot bear to have this thought tearing me up, putting me together, knowing that all that I desire is nonsense, perfectly clear. I need to untwist this knot and then tie it again.

"I must quickly write this book to help others find ways of praising me. I want all the undivided support with admiration, while to give nothing in return. I want nothing. I want them all to despise me. I want to be at the bottom of existence but to still compliment large people in swimsuits. I want anxiety and fear. I want a horrible existence. I will settle for what I get because I am worthy of so much more. I cannot stop this avalanche of joy, and I know there is something inside of me that is unworthy, something awful making me great..."

# 11 Religion:
## Justifying its Place in an Empirical World

*A little philosophy inclineth a man's mind to atheism;
but depth in philosophy bringeth men's
minds about to religion.*
—FRANCES BACON

Emily embraces the laws of physics, Darwin's theory, Euclid's geometry, and the periodic chart of elements. Every knowable thought necessarily reduces to facts demonstrable by experimentation. Newton's laws of motion explain the earth's rotation around the sun in an observable way. These same equations describe dropping a ball in a vacuum, precisely predicting its location, velocity, and acceleration. In addition, the force exerted on the ball by the earth's gravity effectively establishes its mass.

Emily wastes little time in church since God has no experimental method by which one determines his existence. No scale measures his height, no logical theory explains his thought processes, and no camera photographs him or any other mythological beings. Emily respects only hard repeatable evidence as confirmation of anything. Emily lists Galileo and Louis Pasteur, along with John Watson and Francis Crick, among her apostles; she decrees sainthood on Freud, Thomas Edison, Alexander Bell, and others.

She agrees with psychologists who often subtly refute the authenticity of God, knowing that, at best, religion makes believers happy the way Santa Claus brings children smiles on Christmas morning. At worst, religion forces the ignorant sinner to recoil with fear of a nonexistent prudish god, who, according to the Bible, tortures the unfaithful for all eternity. The afterlife? Heaven and hell are one in the same, consisting of formaldehyde dispersed throughout the body and of worms crawling inside the brain. Life after death equates to magic frogs chasing leprechauns.

Psychology, unlike religion, describes the world in useful ways. To Emily, pain and pleasure decide the direction the brain travels, not the Holy Ghost. Condition, combined with experience, genetics, and environment, predict behavior, not free will. The determined existence of Emily requires no concept of choosing, just biological connections inside the brain guiding thoughts.

The lack of respect empiricism receives infuriates this thirty-two-year-old technophile. The stupidity of the masses who spend money on churches, fortunetellers, astrology, and voodoo boggles her mind. All of it would make her laugh, but she cares about these idiots. Why can't they see the world as molecules, atoms, and electrons? Why rely on ancient superstition, instead of the mind's reasoning abilities?

Emily studies the brain's structure as well as how it functions, wishing to convince everyone of their own ability to discover a world superior to folklore and crystal balls. Emily knows the advantages of empirical thought will one day cut through the fog of ignorance.

By observation she reluctantly, indeed angrily, concludes that the human mind posses the tools necessary to lie to itself. How else could the religious dolts deny evolution in favor of ancient fairy tales? Why choose to die a martyr for a fictitious god? What justifies Christian sacrifice when everybody eventually turns to dust? Emily recognizes that she must tell the world about the benefits of molecular biology and quantum mechanics. She reasons that people can pick illogical paths to follow, and therefore her place in the world is promoting clear, sound judgment.

Emily's ultimate justification for correcting others, derives from a sense of accomplishment she feels when teaching them to find the obvious truth. In addition, every time an unlearned fool comes out of darkness and into the scientific community, Emily receives praise from her freethinking friends. (Freethinking in this case means free of God.) She accepts the praise because it only motivates her to do more good, thereby making the world better still.

## But Why?

To be fair, Emily (the ever-inquiring extremist) begins to question the motives of the empiricists. "I love and trust the scientific method, but is there a reason?" she asks. Emily seeks a philosophical justification. Since a cause exists for everything, then faith in science too requires an explanation—or maybe several. Emily accepts that she strives for happiness as a fundamental motive and that happiness is good—the more the better. Perhaps there are minor complications; for example, her sophistication allows for the realization that short-term gratification is less important than long-term. Nonetheless, she seeks to increase joyful prosperity today as well as everyday hereafter until death at an old age. Without a God to judge, she relies on her own perceptions to maximize enjoyment. And if that were not enough, empirically derived knowledge increases pleasure, verified, of course, by observation. Understanding human nature demonstrates that empiricism promotes good, or pleasure, and reduces evil, or pain.

Emily created her philosophy in this manner; however, all philosophy is doublethink. Therefore she cannot deny the following.

If empirical knowledge sometimes guides the thoughts in Emily's head, if the laws of physics expounded by Isaac Newton, Albert Einstein, and the rest, convince this same woman to behave in a certain manner, if the justification for people living the way they do is to reduce anguish and fear, at the same time increase joy, and this is deemed good, then Emily must concede that beyond a doubt, the following is also true:

If religious people live their lives at least roughly in accordance with their beliefs in God, if some of the ideas in a mind are guided by thoughts about the Father in heaven, if the laws as expounded by Moses, Jesus, and others convince a person to behave in a certain manner, if a person acts the way they do in order to reduce anguish and fear at the same time increase joy, then the existence of God is as much a certainty as any logical system, empiricism, or hedonism.

If trigonometry, computers, and psychology are deemed useful based on their contributions to the betterment of mankind, then by a similar principle we should evaluate the Father, Son, and Holy Ghost. Psychology tells us that movements in the brain's cells make a difference, and that affecting a person's behavior is real. Thus, seeing a brick wall on the outside of a bank establishes a mental image containing the properties of a solid boundary and indicates to our brain synapses that the money inside is not for anyone to help themselves to. In a similar vein, if a person's belief in God prevents robbing a bank by forming an image roughly comparable to a physical barrier, then the belief in God is as real as the one made by viewing bricks and mortar. If we accept the validity of solid object's existence, then we must also accept the validity of an individual's fear of God.

If the motivation for wanting our children to become happy and productive members of society makes us support their seventh grade science teacher, then by the same rationale, we should have them believe their religious instructors on Sunday. Additionally, if we consider the results of an empirical study valid because it causes a shift in patterns of thought to a more pleasant state, then we must accept God when he too changes people to a more pleasant state. If students read and accept a book on relativity as real because it moves their understanding of science to a more useful state, then sensibility also tells students to act that way with respect to the Bible when it provides a similarly useful education about living.

If the threat of a lawsuit for illegal behavior prevents the citizens of Emily's hometown of Dubuque, Iowa, from harming their neighbors, and if knowledge of a lawsuit comes via stimuli and causes a fearful rage, then only a stubborn idiot regards the fear of God as any less meaningful than a lawsuit. Scientific methods lead to the inevitable conclusion that knowledge of the world comes through sense stimuli to the brain, and if the mind perceives God, and this perception affects the mind's memories and actions, then God exists and is real.

Anatomy, biology, and chemistry describe the mind as consisting of chemical reactions causing electron movements. Psychologists treat anything stirring the thoughts in our head as real since they alter our lives. Thus a memory about Madam Curie puts our mind in motion, just the same as a memory of God's Ten Commandments. Furthermore, if knowledge of God, including his perfection and omnipotence, also inspires awe and joy, then humankind knows the reality of his greatness. The mind's knowledge of an omnipotent being in part persuades the heart that there is an afterlife, hence there is one. Furthermore, people are obligated by the laws of empiricism to act accordingly. Because a jealous God exists, man must arrange his beliefs to exclude all other gods. In fact, he must order his thoughts such that these other gods no longer exist. There is just one God. God tells man that mortal ideas can be wrong and we should trust his judgment universally. If carbon dating conflicts with God's word, then trust the Bible alone.

The study of geometry and architecture allows for the construction of great buildings. Furthermore, proof that Euclidean truths extend beyond the mind of man is exhibited by the existence of skyscrapers. By the same token thoughts of God have been inside the head of many men, and in turn it caused them to build great cathedrals; therefore, we know God exists outside of men's heads the same as a geometric proof.

The concept of a perpetual motion machine confuses some students of physics, and this ignorance causes them to foolishly try to build such a contraption—in some cases exhausting all worldly possessions in the pursuit of a physical impossibility. By parallel logic, if the existence of people of different faiths confuses a believer, and prevents him or her from experiencing joyful clumps, then another's false faith is no more legitimate than a perpetual motion machine.

If Darwin's theory of evolution explains nature while helping its followers feel more confident and reassured, and if the existence of trees and birds seems miraculous proof of a wonderful God, then the existence of the Almighty is no less certain than the theory of evolution. And if the theory of evolution's conflicts with the Bible cause a significant threat to a person's serenity, then it might as well go the way of the dinosaur. And if doublethink philosophy and modern psychology seem too much based on human values instead of God's laws contained in the Bible, such that a person's core values become confused, then the notion of doublethink and psychoanalysis belong in Satan's domain. And if the belief in eternal life and God's judgment require free will, a believer can be as certain of free will as the sun rising in the east tomorrow morning.

Even though religion profoundly affects the minds of believers, there is clearly no guarantee that faith alone always prevents the formation of, as well as visits to, thoughts and actions of the evil unpleasant type. However, God's teachings often help establishing spiritual and physical lifestyles that cause less anxious uncertainty. While psychoanalysis encourages the exploration of painful memories to improve our mental health, religion utilizes various means to make some of the most awful thoughts inaccessible or moot. Religion takes on some painful transgressions directly; such is the case when one confesses his sins to God. The net effect of religion is an extremely powerful tool in dealing with the doubts lying inside of our heads. A direct commandment from God such as, "Thou shall not commit adultery," reduces a woman's need to seek the illicit sexual fulfillment. God's ability to destroy an entire city makes decisions about sin easier, simpler, even clearer.

Sometimes doublethink philosophy confuses and misleads. By contrast the Bible's recorded words of Jesus Christ are not twisted or perverted to logical extremes. When Jesus says that it is better to pluck an eye out than to lust after someone else's wife, it squelches the debate among his followers. The Holy Bible, when embraced without fear or trepidation, allows the human mind to happily accept a lifestyle filled with love and joy. Although Christianity may be philosophically equivalent to believing in the spiritual power of toads, there is little evidence of wart worshipers finding peaceful contentment.

Why write a book that denounces the philosophical underpinnings of religion and then encourages the blind acceptance of Christianity? Because even though there is no philosophical reason for God to exist, many millions happily embrace him. God lives despite man's reasoning ability. The study of philosophy ultimately leads nowhere, but by default we must draw the following conclusions:

- There is no need to justify one's belief in unexplainable events like creation.
- There is no need to reconcile the Bible to the world.
- There is no need to explain perceived biblical lapses in logic.

- There is no philosophical need to defend one's faith in God.

Confusion that one might have in his or her faith is not evidence in the incorrectness of the Bible. An inability to comprehend God's plan for the world is not a proof for atheism. Doublethink (absurdity) is not a credible threat against God unless the door is left open. Stating evil is good does not make it so. The beliefs of those who do not follow the teachings of the Lord are irrelevant to the truth. It is possible to trick or confuse one's understanding of the value system of Christ, as well as all the potential replacement value systems.

Although no philosophical link connects this chapter to the rest of the book, there is no such thing as philosophical consistency. It is however possible to have beliefs that allow a person the ability to embrace various inconsistencies contained herein, as well as retain their sanity, happiness—and their love of God. What types of existence are desired? If a person wants stability, extended joy, peaceful coexistence, and happiness, that individual should consider religion, and in particular, the following.

**Prayer:** Permits a believer to talk to someone without the socially constraining hangups that negative reactions from other people cause. Prayer helps the believer visit his or her innermost thoughts in a nonthreatening manner, even when they are ordinarily difficult to find.

**Omnipotent God:** Keeps a person out of behaviors that disagree with religion. Keeps a person from considering acts such as murder, rape, stealing, and lying.

**"Thou shall not steal":** Taking another person's belongings tends to cause rage as well as other extreme emotions. A thieving society leads to unstable intense mental states such as fear or resentment, and actions that ultimately produce more unpleasant stimuli.

**"Thou shall not covet thy neighbor's wife":** Same as above.

**"Thou shall not murder":** Same as above.

**"Thou shall not commit adultery":** A stable, committed relationship can promote a pleasant manner of being. If a man loves his wife, and she is also a close friend, is not excessively judgmental, loves back, and even provides sexual gratification, then he can expect to find a lifestyle high in pleasant stimulation and a happier existence.

**"Love thy neighbor as thyself":** Encourages social stability.

In essence, religion provides a life-management system demonstrating great successes. Those individuals who choose to forgo religion are often greatly disappointed by the results, because there are no readily available alternatives in place. The morals developed by most nonreligious philosophers do not even come close to governing relationships and personal behavior in a productive manner. These atheistic philosophies consist of notions of Communism and fluff, propagated by those ill-suited to religion. Being against religion does not demonstrate a better way. Freud's writings and philosophy implied that somehow science would soon resolve mental conflicts in a far more efficient manner than religion. Freud was wrong.

# 12 *Free Will*

According to astronomers and mathematicians, we know the earth travels around the sun, and likewise, the moon about the earth. The equations for the planet's wobbling elliptical orbit, as well as the axial spinning of a spherical mass in twenty-four hour increments, are explained conveniently by Newton's laws of motion, Gottfried Liebniz's calculus, Nicolaus Copernicus's observations, Einstein's modern physics, and so on.

But I too can make observations and theories on the nature of the earth and its relation to sun and moon. First of all, the ground I walk on is not spherical at all. Beyond a shadow of a doubt here where I live in northeast Iowa, it is quite uneven, hilly, covered with different vegetation, houses, farms, roads, streets, people, and animals. When someone tells me the earth is a big ball, I am inclined to question their sanity. Indeed these "scientists" seem inclined to stating the earth is this near perfect shape to make a gross oversimplification to more easily explain the math and physics.

In addition, most days I see the amber morning sun glowing dimly above my neighbor's yard across the street. As I travel to work, it follows me about, usually changing to a brighter yellow, also feeling warmer around the middle of the day. I suspect the sun is pancake-shaped, but I am not certain. When I hear the earth spins about an axis running roughly between its poles, and then that the sun rests in a relatively fixed position, I am quite perplexed, as I am not dizzy and have never had any reason to believe that I am turning at hundreds or thousands of miles per hour. No, the scientific explanation is way too convoluted and useless, because I know for a fact the sun travels across the sky changing in color and intensity throughout the day, as well as hiding behind clouds.

The moon, on the other hand, pops up at all different times and shapes, usually during the night. It is a semi-randomly positioned object moving through the sky. That is my law of lunar motion and thus far my law is a hundred percent correct and always obeyed. With so much confidence, I am emboldened to create a second law: When the moon is round and visible one night, you'll often see it again the following night with the same shape. Other times it disappears for weeks on end. If the scientists are able to approximate the shape of the earth, then I too can approximate the behavior of the moon.

In general, the scientists are too lazy, stupid, or incompetent to explain common phenomenon, in a manner better than I. We can be certain that the earth is at least partially hilly and jagged where I live; the sun and moon pass over my home (not the other way around) and the moon is semi-random in its behavior.

Scientists are fundamentally narrow-minded. They choose laws and formulas to promote and simplify their own biased outlooks. They find it far too great a burden to explain a star moving across the sky billions of light years away in not easily defined patterns at speeds perhaps many orders of magnitude faster than the speed of light. (Which is roughly what I see on the nights I look.) They scoff at the ancient Christian belief that the flat earth is at the center of the universe but offer only ever more difficult explanations of orbits and gravity. They search for the most elegant and pure calculation, and then proclaim it the absolute, undeniable, and empirically verifiable truth.

They prefer to deny the randomness of the moon, instead favoring a concise set of formulas dictating its behavior. The moon, they say, is governed by calculus and geometric patterns. While not agreeing with them, I can use their methodology, follow their lead, and bias my outlook to my own personal needs. I do not give a hoot where the moon is tonight or next week either. My method is far simpler and fits my own narrow-minded purposes. The moon is a semi-random object, occasionally showing up two days in a row. Its shape changes, and the color varies as well; that is all I ever need, elegant as can be.

But I am deceiving you a bit, since I really don't care about the follies of science regarding the solar system but used their silliness to illustrate a point. I care far more about what I am told are the "scientific" explanations for my behavior, and the belief that the laws of chemistry, physics, and cellular biology govern me. Although psychologists must admit there are a number of gaps in their current understanding of the human mind, many *educated* fools will still insist that I can no more break the fundamental principles put forth by the great scientists of old and new than I could walk off the edge of the world.

Just as in the instance of the earth, moon, and sun, I once again find the scientists brashly choosing to ignore the obvious, for I am the initiator of my actions. When I want an apple from a tree, I grab it and eat it. Pure and simple, elegant as can be. In this case, I admit I may be as lazy as they are since I do not have the energy to pursue a scientific theory involving math, physics, chemistry, biology, physiology, and psychology. I just want the apple, so I extend my arm into the branches, pull down a red macintosh, and place it in my mouth. This new theory works, and works very well.

You could say I have free will. In fact, free will is the most simple and elegant method for explaining my behavior. I do what I want to do.

If the "great" geniuses are biased toward writing formulas in their simplest form, then I am the brightest thinker of all time because I can account for my own behavior. And even if they should ever fill in the gaps in their extraordinarily elaborate models, they cannot account for my actions in a more useful manner than my willing it freely.

Yes, I have free will more certainly than the earth is round.

# Afterthought: More Background

*When I was a small child, my mother told me, "God is everywhere," to which I replied, "Even in a light bulb?"*
—RICK WEIRES

In my youth I did not realize I had philosophies. At six years of age the plan was something like this: I attended services in a beautiful church with an overwhelming organ. I never doubted the existence of God, I wanted to be bigger, and I liked candy and balloons. My thinking back then lacked consistency, failing to prioritize my likes, fears, and beliefs into a coherent world view.

I gradually found some hierarchy; mainly I sought to not have the same confining values my parents had. Like most teenagers I struggled to find things they were right about. (The doublethink philosophy and age eventually explained their behavior and straightened out so many other things as well. Now I admire my parents.)

Throughout school and college, I developed complex systems for determining right from wrong. This helped me avoid conflicts, arguments, and disputes—not because they were evil or wrong, but because I could not deal with the anger in others. I still fear people will not like what I say and anticipate some will hate me if they know what I really think.

At one time my politics were very liberal and rather silly. My leftward leanings were based on fear that if I did not treat others well, then I was nothing in society. I grew angry because friends, fellow students, and coworkers did not accept what I knew was right. I made efforts, but they were seldom perceived or rewarded as I thought they should be.

I was against religion (but not anymore). Frequently, I felt nothing, empty. I read many books, but just two authors continued to captivate my thoughts: Dostoyevsky and Freud. They both looked life in the eye and took what it had to offer. If life was miserable, then at least we finally knew. Their intellectual integrity, or at least the ability to ignore conventional thoughts, intrigued me. I knew the world made no sense and yet I was unable to accept the world even if it did. I was miserable at times but finally settled on at least one worthy goal: to avoid ridicule. What that specifically meant was achieving a philosophy beyond reproach. Although it seems silly now, I succeeded in two ways:

1. Doublethink is a baseless philosophy, depriving any criticism directed at me of a foundation.

2. My own irrational exaggerated fear clumps provided a prime motive for developing doublethink. Once created, intentional doublethink destroyed many nonsensical and unneeded painful clumps, while forcing me to address condemnation directly. It turns out that outside critique is not so bad. In other words, doublethink made others' harsh judgments more tolerable for me.

Once freed of many unpleasant and painful clumps, I built back a new clump system. The new me became happier, more mature, and focused. For the first time I developed a belief system closely suited to my actual needs. Then it dawned on me: the power of doublethink. I knew it was not only a philosophical aberration but also a great psychological cleanser. Earlier I so doubted that anything useful would ever come from the doublethink idea, I pursued it mainly because intellectual integrity refused to let it go. I found such a gray area at the beginning that I might have followed Nietzsche into insanity. I could not have known my destination at the start of doublethink. But unlike poor Nietzsche, the lack of a formal philosophy provided me an acceptable alternative.

Dale Carnegie also influenced me in numerous ways. I first read *How to Win Friends and Influence People* about twenty years ago. While I have never heard him called an existentialist, he showed a trait that links some existentialists. He never needed philosophical justification; he simply wanted to create happiness and did so. After first reading him, I underestimated Carnegie, viewing him as shallow, lacking the insight of Freud and Dostoyevsky. But at the same time I never let go of the simple Carnegie principles, one of which made me question my own unhappiness. I reasoned that the world made no sense, so why not allow happiness? I hated being miserable, and he made life pleasant. He helped save me.

Near the end of this writing I finally attended the Dale Carnegie course. I will never underestimate him again. He provided the catalyst to finish this book. His teachings pushed me into a vision of writing, improved my personal relationships (which allowed me to write), and finally energized me to complete the process. I shall forever reside in his debt.

# References

Freud, Sigmund. *The Cambridge Companion to Freud*. Edited by Jerome Nue. Reprint, Cambridge: Cambridge University Press. [1900] 1999.

Hall, Calvin. *A Primer of Freudian Psychology*. New York: Meridian. [1954] 1999.

Marx, Karl, and Friedrich Engels. *The Communist Manifesto*. Edited by Samuel H. Beer. New York: Meredith Corporation. [1848] 1955.

Nietzsche, Friedrich. *Untimely Meditations*. Edited by Daniel Breazeale. Translated by R. J. Hollingdale. Cambridge: Cambridge University Press. [1873–76] 1997.

———*Thus Spoke Zarathustra*. Translated by Walter Kaufmann. New York: Penguin Books. [1892] 1978.

———*The Gay Science*. Edited by Bernard Williams. Translated by Josefine Nauckhoff. Cambridge: Cambridge University Press. [1882] 2001.

Orwell, George. *1984*. New York: Signet Classics. [1949] 1983.

Sartre, Jean-Paul. *Being and Nothingness*. Translated by Hazel E. Barnes. First Pocket Books printing. New York: Washington Square Press. [1956] 1966.

# Index

# Give the Gift of
# *The Philosophy of Doublethink*
## to Your Friends and Colleagues

### CHECK YOUR LEADING BOOKSTORE OR ORDER HERE

❑ **YES**, I want _____ copies of *The Philosophy of Doublethink* at $16.95each, plus $4.95 shipping per book (Iowa residents add $1.19 sales tax per book; Ohio residents add $1.23 sales tax per book.) Canadian orders m1ust be accompanied by a postal money order in U.S. funds. Allow 15 days for delivery.

❑ **YES**, I am interested in having Rick Weires speak or give a seminar to my company, association, school, or organization. Please send information.

My check or money order for $_____ is enclosed.

Please charge my:   ❑ Visa    ❑ MasterCard
                   ❑ Discover   ❑ American Express

Name _____

Organization _____

Address _____

City/State/Zip _____

Phone_____ E-mail _____

Card # _____

Exp. Date_____ Signature _____

*Please make your check payable and return to:*
**Bookmasters, Inc.**
2541 Ashland Road • Mansfield, OH 44905
## Call your credit card order to: 800-537-6727
Fax:419-589-4040